THE NATURAL DEPRAVITY
OF MANKIND

THE NATURAL DEPRAVITY OF MANKIND

Observations on the Human Condition
by Ferdinand Lundberg

BARRICADE BOOKS INC.
NEW YORK

Published by Barricade Books Inc.
61 Fourth Avenue
New York, NY 10003

Printed in the United States of America.

Library of Congress Cataloging-in-Publication Data

Lundberg, Ferdinand, 1902–
    The natural depravity of mankind / by Ferdinand Lundberg.
       p.   cm.
    ISBN 1-56980-003-0: $15.95
       1. Man.   2. World politics—20th century.   3. Moral conditions.
    I. Title.
    BD450.L8   1994   93-40407
    128—dc20   CIP

First printing

To the memory of David Hume
1711-1776

THE NATURAL DEPRAVITY OF MANKIND

By Ferdinand Lundberg

Man is not only the most versatile animal on earth—endlessly eulogized by professors of philosophy and hailed as God's chief handiwork by theologians—but he is also the most dangerous—to himself, his fellows and to all other animals. The experience of the twentieth century proves this beyond doubt. For it has been the century of the most profligate slaughter and destruction, all to no purpose.

As this report is being written, scattered replications of the century's carnage are being staged all over the globe—in the Balkans, the Middle East, Somalia, the Sudan, India, South Africa, northern Ireland, among others. In major cities around the world there are startling events: fantastic bombings in New York City and London, politico-religious assassinations here and there, as in Egypt, India and Sri Lanka, disaffection on every hand. At the same time civilian crime is mushrooming everywhere.

The chief means of most of this destruction has been military action by governments. Governments both dictatorial and elective have played the major role. These governments in all cases have been in the control of a few men. In no case has any nation ever gone to war after a national plebiscite.

In anybody's hands government is always a potential danger, a fact well understood by the writers of the United States Constitution. In this century government, to its disrepute, has been freely used contrary to the interests of the masses, in harmony only with the suppositions of the rulers of the moment.

The lesson, if any, therefore, is: "Be on guard with respect to all acts of government, especially military acts." Even worse than what has been seen may be in store for helpless humanity with the widening distribution of nuclear weapons.

Governments, of course, are not independent mechanisms or automatons although they may seem so from the outside. They are always directed by specifically designated men, and are the chief instruments of such men. So, blame for all the destruction cannot be heaped on governments in the abstract but must fall upon the men in charge and upon those who empowered these men.

That is, the blame for all the carnage and destruction of the twentieth century must fall on the shoulders of specific men and their willing supporters.

The title of this book is a phrase in an essay by the great British philosopher David Hume (1711-1776), one he entitled "That Politics May Be Reduced To A Science."[1]

In it Hume wrote: "In the smallest court or office, the stated forms and methods by which business must be conducted are found to be a considerable check on the natural depravity of mankind."

Hume was not referring to heads of government but to everybody without exception. What he meant by the depravity was explained in an earlier work, *A Treatise of Human Nature* (1739-1740), on which his fame chiefly rests. He also wrote a six-volume *History of England*, from the invasion of Julius Caesar to 1688; *Enquiry Concerning Human Understanding; Enquiry Concerning the Principles of Morals; Dialogues Concerning Natural Religion*, and other influential works that are still being published.

"Nothing is more certain," Hume wrote "than that men are, in a great measure, governed by interest, and that even when they extend their concern beyond themselves, 'tis not to any great distance; nor is it usual for them, in common life, to look farther than their nearest friends and acquaintance. 'Tis no less certain, that 'tis impossible for men to consult their interest in so effectual a manner, as by an universal and inflexible observance of the rules of justice, by which alone they preserve society, and keep them-

---

[1] The essay in question may be found at page 295 and the quoted phrase at page 302 of *Hume's Political and Moral Philosophy*, edited by Prof. Henry D. Aiken, of Harvard University, Hafner Publishing Co., N.Y., 1948.

selves from falling into that wretched and savage condition, which is commonly represented as the *state of nature.*"

In this state of nature, as Thomas Hobbes noted in the previous century, life was nasty, brutish and short. The state of affairs in Somalia in the early 1990s would approximate it.

Men, Hume argued, have dual interests—first their personal interest in whatever their projects or enterprises are and then their general or collective interest in being guided by the rules of justice and equity enforced by their government. Man, however, has a more vivid sense of personal interest and a much weaker sense of collective interest, leading him to neglect the latter.

Mankind, Hume went on, assigns the enforcement of the rules of justice and equity to a certain group called magistrates and officers of government. While the rules may be dim to the generality, they are of first importance to these magistrates, who only rarely find them in conflict with their own personal interests.

Governments develop out of this specialized interest in enforcing the laws.

Hume did not see mankind deliberately violating the laws that benefited them. He saw men as simply having a less vivid sense of the laws than of their own projects, whatever they were. The law was remote while the work at hand, whatever it was, had a greater hold on the attention and interest.

While the observation of the laws and the projects in hand was of equal importance to man, in most instances observance of the laws was slighted in favor of matters at hand. Hume felt this was the great weakness of human nature vis-a-vis society.

And while Hume in his *A Treatise of Human Nature* referred only to the rules of governmment, his vision applies equally to all traditional rules governing human behavior, whatever their source: religious, moral or political.

Warfare itself clearly signifies a breakdown of civilized society as between nations. The resort to force at once puts the parties on the same footing as people in a state of nature. Within a society, men who violate the law are clearly attacking that society. When one society attacks another it is clearly reverting to a state of nature, to the rule of fang and claw.

Despite all talk of human progress, this century has seen far more violence, national and international, than ever before. As far as violence is concerned, the scene grows worse instead of better.

While Hume is unquestionably correct about the general process and motivation in forming governments, his observations have a somewhat old-fashioned ring. They do not take account of modern high-tech dictatorships and so-called democracies in which governments fail to conform to the ideal mold presented by the sagacious Hume.

Hume was through and through a government man, believing that any government was better than no government. One can agree with Hume here when one considers what happens in the absence of government, such as in Somalia in the early 1990s. Destructive anarchy ensues. But Hume could not anticipate that governments would some day turn themselves into instruments of wholesale rapine, destruction and loot. Or that governments would be converted, either in whole or in part, into instruments of injustice.

Before leaving this aspect of his topic, Hume stresses emphatically: "There is no quality in human nature, which causes more fatal errors in our conduct, than that which leads us to prefer whatever is present to the distant and remote, and makes us desire objects more according to their situation than their intrinsic value."

Hume points out that justice consists of three principal parts: the stability of possession, its transfer by consent and the performance of promises as in contracts. Government ensures all of these and, in the event of disputes, it adjudicates them and will punish those who break the rules of justice.

Hume also said:

"The same self-love, therefore, which renders men so incommodious to each other, taking a new and more convenient direction, produces the rules of justice, and is the first motive of their observance."[2]

"We blame all treachery and breach of faith because

---

[2] *Ibid.* p. 543

The Natural Depravity of Mankind

we consider that the freedom and extent of human commerce depend entirely on a fidelity with regard to promises. We blame all disloyalty to magistrates because we perceive that the execution of justice, in the stability of possession, its translation by consent, and the performance of promises is impossible without submission to government."[3]

"When men submit to the authority of others, 'tis to procure themselves some security against the wickedness and injustice of men, who are perpetually carried by their unruly passions, and by their present and immediate interest, to the violation of all the laws of society."[4]

". . . whenever the civil magistrate carries his oppression so far as to render his authority perfectly intolerable, we are no longer bound to submit to it."[5]

". . . we may resist the more violent effects of supreme power, without any crime or injustice."[6]

"As numerous and civilized societies cannot subsist without government, so government is entirely useless without an exact obedience. We ought always to weigh the advantages which we reap from authority, against the disadvantages; and by this means we shall

---

[3] *Ibid.* p. 546
[4] *Ibid.* p. 551
[5] *Ibid.* p. 551
[6] *Ibid.* p. 552

become more scrupulous of putting in practice the doctrine of resistance."[7]

". . . there scarce is any race of kings, or form of a commonwealth, that is not primarily founded on usurpation and rebellion, and whose title is not at first worse than doubtful and uncertain."[8]

"Few governments will bear being examined . . . rigorously."[9]

And finally, "the study of history confirms the reasoning of true philosophy which, showing us the original qualities of human nature, teaches us to regard the controversies in politics as incapable of any decision in most cases, and as entirely subordinate to the interests of peace and liberty."[10]

So much for Hume although the reader would be well advised to read his books in their entirety.

Political Developments Since Hume

David Hume died in 1776 at the age of 65. Posthumously he became one of the most commented upon philosophers in history and it was Immanuel Kant who said "Hume awoke me from my dogmatic slumbers." But political events, far from refuting Hume,

---

[7] *Ibid.* p. 553-4
[8] *Ibid.* p. 556
[9] *Ibid.* p. 558
[10] *Ibid.* p. 562

developed in such a way as to show that he had severely underestimated the capacity of mankind for depraved behavior.

We may pass over the American and French revolutions, the Napoleonic wars, the Bourbon restoration in France, and the rule of the Bonapartists and the Franco-Prussian war, not that they do not deserve comment but that the significant departure from the past is the first World War. This war, which was integral to making the 20th century by far the most brutal and ghastly in history, set the stage for events even more fearful in connection with World War II.

All in all, the two world wars destroyed the world that existed at the beginning of the 20th century, leaving it very problematic where it is now headed. The big question is: will the 21st century be better or worse for humanity?

It is hard to believe but the various declarations of war in 1914 by the European Powers were the consequences of rational calculations by the various governments. These governments thought in terms of old-style wars, little reckoning on the vast amount of destructive power now at the disposal of any government as a consequence of the Industrial Revolution. Every European government, except possibly that of Russia, possessed the industrial power single-handedly to destroy Europe and possibly the entire world. And this was long before the advent of the atomic bomb.

First Austria-Hungary declared war on Serbia in

retaliation for the assassination of the Austrian crown prince at Sarajevo. Russia, a Slavic partisan of Serbia, responded by ordering full mobilization of its peasant hordes. Germany, which had tacitly supported Austria in its claims on Serbia, reacted to the Russian mobilization by ordering its own full mobilization.

France now mobilized in defense against the German mobilization and Britain momentarily hesitated before joining France. Italy also joined in the fray, switching sides at the last minute from Germany, Austria and Turkey.

The lines of the conflict had now been decided. They were to be France, Britain, Italy and Russia against Germany, Austria-Hungary and Turkey. After the war there was much debate on who had been most responsible for plunging the continent into devastating war. Actually all the governments were equally guilty, planning for precisely this outcome.

The British cabinet hesitated the longest about joining in the war and it held the key to whether it was to be a purely European war or a world war. As the cabinet hesitated, it was importuned by a prominent Britisher, Bertrand Russell, not to enter the war. Although Russell was already a distinguished mathematician and philosopher he was no mere individual in the mass of citizens. Although not a member of the government Russell was a member of a long-distinguished aristocratic family and he was giving the government salutary advice.

Russell's objections were ignored and he was rebuffed as a pacifist, a word of sinister meaning to all governments bent on war. And as Russell objected to conscription after Britain entered the war he was arrested, tried and jailed for six months, thus quelling the one prominent voice that could have saved Britain and the British empire.

The British cabinet of 1914 was in fact being advised by an aristocratic insider who was a leading world philosopher of the twentieth century not to enter upon a self-destructive course.

Russell's insight was so superior to that of the government that it does not bear comparison. Later, commenting on what would have happened had Britain not entered the war, Russell conceded that Germany would have defeated France, imposed an indemnity as in 1871 and then gone home. Millions of German, French and English lives would have been spared.

That Russell was no rigid pacifist ideologue was shown in the 1930s when he did not object to arming to oppose Hitler.

Because Germany first launched its mobilized forces against France and Russia it was widely regarded in the United States as the aggressor. But the German authorities knew that both the French and Russian governments had long been plotting to encircle Germany militarily and thus defeat it with the collaboration of Great Britain and its mighty empire.

Germany, for its part, since its unification in 1870, had looked with envy at Britain and France, the two most successful predatory powers in the world. It sought to emulate them in every way, especially by the seizure of foreign territories. In this mutually vicious rivalry France probably showed the most animus as it was motivated by a strong spirit of revenge for its defeat by Germany in 1870-1.

Russia's motivation was to protect its Slavic partners in the Balkans and Britain's was to play its historic role of intervening against the stronger force on the continent. This policy of Britain's had until now enabled it to survive. For Britain had been twice invaded and totally subjugated, first by Julius Caesar and then by William the Conqueror of Normandy, and had twice been threatened with invasion, first by Spain and then by Napoleon.

In fact, everybody in Europe had reasons to fear their neighboring countries. Since the time of the early Greeks and Romans every government in Europe, large or small, had been either a predator or the victim of a predator. The reason for this is not that Europeans are peculiarly vicious; for the same state of affairs has prevailed on other continents from the tribal stage on upward. Men, left to their own devices, simply are not peaceful animals and never were.

A natural advantage the United States has enjoyed is that it occupies a virgin continent that was never allowed to be broken up into small entities and also that it never had to pass through a feudal stage.

World War I caused great harm to Europe and much world dislocation. By the autumn of 1916, it was evident that there was a stalemate on the western front although Russia was cracking on the eastern front. Germany, it appeared, was willing to end the war as a stalemate. France and Great Britain were reluctant to do so even though their losses of men were as great or greater than the losses of the Germans. Why?

For an answer, we must turn to the United States.

The British and the French were reluctant to enter into peace talks with Germany because ever since August, 1914, they had been encouraged by Ambassador Walter Hines Page, U.S. emissary to the Court of St. James, to believe the United States might be brought into the war. Page and President Woodrow Wilson were both ardently and actively pro-British.

It was the prospect of getting the United States into the war that emboldened the British and French to resist attempts at peace. Both nations bent every effort to influence American opinion by lying propaganda. Nearly everything that was said by the British and French about German military behavior was a lie.

The Germans were accused of unrestricted submarine warfare against innocent cargo ships and this was entirely false. For, as later investigation showed, the Germans waged submarine warfare against *armed* merchant vessels carrying contraband cargo, munitions of war.

The situation came about as follows: at the beginning of the war German submarines ordered cargo ships to "stand to" and receive boarding parties, which searched for contraband cargo. If none was found, the ship was allowed to proceed. But if any was found, the ship was sent to a neutral port as a captive or was blown up.

Britain then began secretly arming the ships, which were called "Q ships." With their disguised cannon they could sink any submarine standing by while a searching party was sent. In response to this ruse, the Germans simply took to torpedoing any suspicious-looking ship, which was called unrestricted submarine warfare.

The German sinkings were represented as the sinking of innocent merchantmen and the crews as innocent victims of Teutonic viciousness. Actually, the shoe was on the other foot; it was the British and French who were the vicious ones. The greatest public outrage was expressed over the sinking of the liner *Lusitania*, which carried American passengers who had been warned by Germany in full page advertisements not to travel on the ship as it carried munitions and was a legitimate prey of war. A British court of inquiry held years later confirmed this.

Lying slanders abounded also about the German army, too numerous to detail. One was that the German army on its sweep through Belgium had spitted infants on bayonets and carried them aloft, which would have been foolish for any army to do. Suffice it to say with respect to all the atrocity stories about the German army, that the United States War College at Fort Leavenworth, Kansas, has for years taught senior officers that the German armies in both World

Wars were the greatest and most well-disciplined armies ever to take the field. Those German armies are still the model for the United States army!

But it was as a result of World War I that the power of propaganda was grasped, including the idea that the bigger the lie the more convincing it was. Scores of books have since been written about war propaganda and the techniques of propaganda. Joseph Paul Goebbels as Hitler's Minister of Propaganda put it all to use before and during World War II.

The masters of propaganda have shown that one can persuade the broad public of anything whatever. They can play on the public emotions with the ease of a Horowitz or Paderewski playing the piano. Even Orson Welles with a mild radio sketch about an invasion of beings from outer space unintentionally caused hundreds of panic-stricken people to abandon their homes and flee in cars. The public is ready at any time to be stampeded by authority figures.

Through Wilson's policy of involving the United States in the war out of sympathy for Great Britain, he became the single American in history to do the most harm to the United States, Europe and western civilization. Under Wilson the power of the presidency was used with disastrous consequences.

What Wilson did was to abandon the long-successful policy inaugurated by George Washington, and recommended by him for the future, of never entering into entangling alliances with foreign powers. It was well known back in Washington's time that the

European Powers, ever wrangling and changing sides, were always getting into wars. Even at that time Americans on their own continent had fought against French, Spanish and British forces. But Wilson, for the first time in 125 years, jettisoned this policy and forced the resignation of Secretary of State William Jennings Bryan, who sought to uphold it. And this despite the fact that Bryan had been a chief influence in 1912 in procuring the nomination of Wilson by the Democratic Party.

Wilson's change-over was destructive in several ways. In the first place it led Britain and France to sabotage peace attempts in 1916 in the expectation that with American aid they would be able ultimately to conquer Germany. This policy led to much greater losses of life on both sides, including British and French. By encouraging a continuation of the war, the policy also led the Germans to pound the Russians harder and bring Russia down in 1917. The policy also guaranteed the success of the Bolshevik revolution, which was opposed by the United States to the extent of sending anti-Bolshevik troops to Russia and Siberia.

Again, the policy was costly to the United States, in debt, materials and lives as the United States joined in the war in April, 1917.

How could all this be, as Wilson was the most educated man ever to hold the presidency? A former college professor and president of Princeton University, Wilson was a doctor of philosophy in, of all subjects, political science. One might have thought this would give him great insight as president but his political science had been confined to America exclusively, not to governments and history in general.

But there were profound reasons for Wilson's misjudgments about the war, all concealed from public view. Wilson, it has been established, had long been a very ill man. He had a long carefully concealed history of cerebral vascular disease beginning back in the 1890s. In 1906 it caused him to go blind in his left eye. He was president of Princeton at the time and the fact of his illness was concealed all along. During his presidency his disease caused several episodes of odd behavior owing to an insufficiency of bloodsupply to the brain. He had a predictable stroke in 1919 that left him incapacitated although this fact was also concealed from the public.

The full story of Wilson's long-concealed illness is given by Dr. Edward W. Weinstein, professor of neurology at the Mount Sinai School of Medicine, City University of New York, in a long, detailed article in *The Journal of American History* for September, 1970. I discussed the case at considerable length in my book *Cracks in the Constitution*, 1980.

The Wilson case brought out a defect in the Constitution in that candidates for president are not required to take a physical and mental examination that would show whether or not they were fit for the job. Candidates, in fact, often conceal bad health. Since Wilson at least two presidents have been shown to be seriously ill at the time they took office. Warren G. Harding was a far-gone alcoholic who died in office and John F. Kennedy had Addison's disease as well as a venereal disease. Ailments of all these kinds can impair the patient's judgment. Franklin Roosevelt's condition as a result of polio was downplayed.

Wilson's attending physician through all his illness was Dr. Francis X. Dercum of Philadelphia. Upon Dercum's death it was discovered that all his patient records had been destroyed. Physicians inform me that this is a very unusual procedure; ordinarily, medical records are preserved. The destruction of Dr. Dercum's records contributed to one of the most fateful cover-ups in American history.

The war itself was a political boon to the Wilson Administration in that it provided American industry with massive war orders. This meant employment for millions but it also meant complicity of the United States in the war. And at the time the war began, the United States was slipping into one of its recurrent economic recessions. A full recession at this time would have hurt Wilson's chances for a second term; so the war orders were welcome.

At the beginning of the war, the British and French arranged for large credits with Wall Street bankers; the existence of these credits later brought American support for the British and French because if they lost the war, it was reasoned, they could not repay the loans. Germany initially could have obtained war credits also but proudly declined to ask for them.

This was a capital diplomatic error. German policy during the war was naive in contrast with that of the internationally experienced British and French.

For example, before taking any step in military frightfulness, the Germans announced what they intended to do, as though to frighten opponents; this they did with unrestricted submarine warfare. The British and French, on the other hand, merely did whatever they wanted to, without proclaiming it in advance. The verbal frightfulness of the Germans did them more harm with world public opinion than any action of their opponents.[11]

Germany sought peace in November, 1918, in response to President Wilson's Fourteen Points proposal. Unfortunately for Germany, Wilson was neither to be in charge of the peace conference nor to have much influence in it. The German army withdrew from France. Germany capitulated but the promises of fair-dealing for Germany by Wilson were broken by Britain and France at the peace conference.

The wishes of the ailing Wilson were pretty generally ignored at the peace conference. The Treaty of Versailles as finally drawn harshly punished Germany. It deprived her of all her colonies, which were seized by Britain and France. It then imposed on her

---

[11] A very readable account of the steps that brought the United States into the war was written by C. Hartley Grattan. It was first published in 1929 with the title "Why We Fought."

such heavy indemnities in materials and money that she could never conceivably pay them.

The idea was to punish Germany for having allegedly started the war, a popular notion at the time because the full extent of war casualties was now disclosed with the lifting of wartime censorship. People were appalled at the full extent of the casualties, consisting of mountains of corpses of young men. The allied politicians wanted to deflect any blame from themselves, who were mainly responsible.

Wartime censorship, ostensibly designed to keep vital information from the enemy, is in all countries primarily designed to keep the home population in the dark, ignorant of the blunders and missteps by the government and the great total of casualties. For example, the government of the Soviet Union concealed from the Russian people until 1993 that the defense of Stalingrad in the second World War had cost one million Russian lives.

An analysis of the potential harmful consequences of the peace terms was published in 1919 by John Maynard Keynes, British economist, under the title *The Economic Consequences of the Peace*. Keynes was a member of the British delegation to the peace conference. His analysis, an example of acute forecasting, predicated just about all the major economic difficulties and some of the political upheavals of the next twenty years. The terms of the treaty were a prime preliminary to the great world depression of the

1930s, an event that mystified millions of rank-and-file citizens in all countries.

The Costs and Consequences of World War I

The costs and consequences of World War I were devastating. The total of lives lost by all the belligerents combined was 12,990,570, according to the *Encyclopedia Americana* "World War I," Section 18. Direct costs of the war were $186.3 billion. (Here one should note that all money figures for both world wars should be multiplied 10 or 12 and sometimes 15 times to yield current money values, in order to reflect the deterioration of currency values, another effect of the wars.) Among the indirect costs of the war was the capital value of the lives lost, which was $67.1 billion in terms of 1914-18 dollars. Property loss came to $29.9 billion. Losses of sea-going merchant vessels were 12,398,372 gross tons. Loss in production during the war came to an estimated $45 billion. War relief expenditures came to an even $1 billion. Losses to neutral nations were $1.75 billion.

The aggregate of all costs was $337.98 billion, which in terms of present-day money values comes close to $4 trillion or about the size of the current United States national debt, itself a result of all the wars.

All in all, World War I was the most destructive

war by far ever seen until then in history, thanks to technological advance.

One of the effects of the war, aside from a rolling series of economic dislocations all over, was the trashing of Germany's reputation. Germany in the latter portion of the nineteenth century and the early years of the twentieth century had gained an international reputation for science, learning and prowess in the arts. Americans in search of graduate degrees in science and medicine went to German universities in droves. In the United States, Germans were the most approved of all immigrant groups owing to their industry and sense of lawful order. All this changed overnight in response to Allied propaganda, in which the United States government joined.

While the Germans during the war were accused of sinking defenseless neutral shipping, a falsehood, nothing was said in the press about the deadly British blockade of Germany that caused illness and premature death for children and the elderly. The British blockade impeded the import of foodstuffs and medicines and was the first of many unnoticed blows against the German population, preparing it for the deadly appeal of Hitler and the Nazis under the load of the postwar indemnities.

The monetary indemnity finally imposed on Germany under the Treaty of Versailles was $32 billion, based on her estimated ability to pay. The United States estimate had been for half of this, the British for $10 billion and the French estimate was $100 billion. In addition, much territory was lopped from Germany in Europe as well as her overseas colonies.

The world public seemed surprised to learn that the Austro-Hungarian empire was an unwilling synthesis of many peoples and territories—Slovenes, Croats, Bosnians, Macedoneons, Czechs, Slovaks, Albanians, Magyars and still others. The Russian empire was a similar synthesis of captive peoples, as the world discovered upon the collapse of the Soviet Union in the late 1980s. Germany, too, in part was composed of captive people, non-Germans. Poland, long divided among Russia, Prussia and Austria, was reconstituted after the war.

German payment of the "war guilt" debt finally broke down and with the advent of Adolf Hitler in 1933 the balance was repudiated.

The greatest effect of the war, however, was the overthrow of the Russian czar in 1917 and the creation of the Soviet Union, which was long to be a bugaboo of western Europe. The threat of socialist totalitarianism was the prime excuse for the upthrust of Fascist totalitarianism in Italy in 1923 and Nazi totalitarianism in Germany in 1933.

With these three dictatorships and their many satellites now inflicted on the world, the fallacy of Woodrow Wilson's "war to save the world for democracy" became glaringly apparent. Quite evidently, matters were going from bad to worse. Actually, western civilization was yet to plumb the depths of depravity.

Very probably, the worst effect of the war was the rise to prominence of the various totalitarianisms—Russian, Italian, German, Spanish and their various satellites. The first of these to come into being was the Soviet Union in Russia.

The Bolsheviks took over the Russian government in October, 1917. The czar and his family had already been deposed in a spontaneous revolution of the army, the peasantry and the city workers. A provisional government with an elected legislature was installed. The Bolsheviks under Lenin attacked and overthrew this government with the slogan "peace and bread." For the provisional government planned to continue the war.

The losses of the poorly-led Russian army were stupendous and that army was often without necessary supplies, such as ammunition. Czarist officers would order charges against the well-armed Germans by men armed only with bayonets. The Russian government, it turned out, had entered the war without sufficient military stocks. The troops finally no longer could put up with this, left the lines and returned home. There they were met and joined by civilians suffering from the economic dislocations in the domestic sector.

The essence of totalitarianism was unremitting terror directed by secret police who had informers scattered through the populace. Such informers composed a veritable army in all totalitarian countries.

Soon after the Bolsheviks took over the Russian

government in October, 1917, they established the Cheka, a brainchild of Lenin's. Its letters were an acronym for its name in Russian, which was The All-Russian Extraordinary Commission. It professed to combat "counter-revolution, sabotage and speculation." So savage were its actions that, owing to criticisms, the Cheka was terminated in 1922 but instantly replaced by a similar organization with another acronymic name: OGPU. This in time became GPU and then, after another series of name changes, it finished as the KGB. Throughout, it was always the old Cheka in its behavior and Hitler's Gestapo became its mirror-image.

While all the totalitarian police organizations were alert to seize any opponent of the regime, they all had a much broader view of their quarry: large groups of people. It was usually a wholesale batch of victims they were after. There was not much difficulty in the Soviet Union to find people who could be classified under vague terms like counter-revolutionary, saboteur or speculator.

Peasants who were reluctant to go into state-run collective farms could be and were classed as counter-revolutionaries or speculators. Such were either bundled off to labor camps in Siberia, transplanted en masse to desolate regions or shot on the spot. Farms were confiscated for collectivization on the ground that the owners were rich peasants. And to be classified as rich, one needed only to own a horse or a cow. Tens of thousands of people of all kinds were shipped to labor camps, tens of thousands were shot. Often, under Stalin, the aim was merely to terrorize large districts in order to keep them from resisting confiscations.

After Hitler was appointed chancellor in 1933 by the ailing Hindenburg, he was able to greatly increase the ranks of the Brown Shirts by police intimidation. Prior to 1933, the Brown Shirts were voluntary Hitler enthusiasts. But as soon as the Gestapo was formed thousands of rank-and-file socialists and communists became Brown Shirts.

The alternative to switching allegiance was to be shot on the spot. I have often wondered what all those who denounce the Germans for supporting Hitler would have done in that situation. I never heard of anyone who ever won an argument with the secret police in their headquarters. The fact is that a large part of the German population was dragooned or deceived into supporting Hitler. Business leaders, afraid of militant socialists and communists, were Hitler's main sponsors in 1933.

In Russia, people were opposed by the government mainly on the basis of class, often arbitrarily stated. In Germany, people were opposed mainly along racial lines even though they were not active opponents of the regime. This meant that Jews, the bane of Hitler's imagination, were designated for destruction along with political opponents, physical defectives, gypsies and neighboring Slavs.

Throughout the 1930s Hitler became more threatening as he became more popular in Germany with the sharp decline in unemployment. He finally invaded the Rhineland to acclaim at home and dismay abroad; the Rhineland had been demilitarized under the Treaty of Versailles. Britain and France fatally hesitated to challenge him. Hitler then threatened Czechoslovakia, and was somewhat appeased when Great Britain in the person of Prime Minister Neville Chamberlain agreed to its partial dismemberment.

Now, sure that he was on the right track and that Britain and France were cowed, Hitler launched an all-out assault on Poland. This led Britain and France, as guarantors of Poland's borders, to declare war on Germany. And thus was World War II begun.

World War II

There were a number of differences between World War I and World War II. First, World War II was bigger and much more destructive. Secondly, World War II extended to all continents without exception where the first war had been largely confined to Europe. Finally, genocide a la Russe had been added to the military programs so that entire classes and races of people were wiped out.

The extermination of peoples, freely practiced by Russia and Germany, came to be called genocide, a new word. The distinction of having invented genocide goes to the Turks, who slaughtered some $1\frac{1}{2}$

million Armenians in 1915 because they seemed to constitute an obstacle to the prosecution of the war. Genocide was eagerly taken up by the Russian Leninists, who freely practiced it against all opponents, real and imagined. The Russians between 1939 and 1941 slaughtered more than 10,000 Polish officers taken in the joint partition of Poland by Stalin and Hitler who were allied prior to Hitler's sudden attack on the Soviet Union in 1941.

The peak strength of the Allies during the war was 46,871,000 individuals in all branches of military service. The peak strength of the Axis powers was 21,695,000 men: battle deaths of the Allies were 11,371,681 and of the Axis were 5,328,494. These figures do not include civilians, who were simply slaughtered out of hand by the advancing German, Japanese and Russian armies.

Peak strength of the United States was 12,300,000 individuals. Battle deaths of the U.S.S.R. were 7,500,000, of China 2,200,000, of Germany 3,500,000 and of Japan 1,219,000.

Other than battle deaths there were deaths from other causes, such as disease and starvation. And then there were the wounded, some of them paralyzed. For the United States, total military strength during the war was 16,353,659, battle deaths were 292,131, deaths from other causes were 115,197, surviving wounded were 671,801 and captured or missing were 139,709. More or less similar ratios prevailed for other countries.

But battle deaths and wounded were not the whole story of this war, which was also waged against unarmed civilian populations, especially in eastern Europe and Russia by the Germans and in China by the Japanese under the one-man dictatorship of General Hideki Tojo.

The physical and mental suffering inflicted by the Axis forces is beyond comprehension. To this suffering must be added the large number of extermination camps operated by the Soviet Union, the Germans and the Japanese.

The Nazis processed 12 million people through their gas ovens and of these half were Jews, practically all the Jews of Germany and eastern Europe they could corral.

There is probably no accurate figure available of all the civilian dead and injured as a consequence of totalitarianism, whether red, brown or black.[12]

According to *The Academic American Encyclopedia*, the total of military people slain in action including those who died from ancillary causes ranged from 15 to 20 million while the total of civilians killed was 25 million. Part of these totals depends upon estimates because the records of personnel in many countries, especially Russia, China and Germany, were destroyed or non-existent. In short, the war itself destroyed much of the evidence of its own destructiveness.

---

[12] *Encyclopedia Americana*, "World War II," section 17.

The same source reports that expenditures for war materials and armaments amounted to $1.154 trillion but no authentic figure exists for the value of property destroyed. In Germany, Russia, China and Japan whole cities were destroyed. By the end of the war most of Germany was a pile of rubble and junk. In Japan two cities were erased by the atomic bomb while half of Tokyo was razed by continuous strategic bombing. The material destruction was incalculable.

Vistas of Totalitarianism

Karl Marx set forth in his writings that the fatal flaw in the human condition, productive of most human social ills, was the existence of private property. It was about private property that capitalists contended and led their governments to contend in imperialist wars. Thus, the thing to do was to get rid of private property: place all productive property under the state ownership and eliminate the detestable capitalists.

This is precisely what Lenin did after the Bolsheviks seized power. For good measure he abolished institutionalized religion on the ground that it was a support for capitalism.

All this was the prescription according to Marx except that it was applied in the wrong place. For Marx had stipulated that the Marxist revolution was to take place only in the most advanced industrial countries, which meant Britain and Germany. Lenin, however, felt it was necessary to act wherever opportunity offered and by acting in industrially backward Russia he would inspire the German workers to rise and establish the Marxist state in Germany. However, the German workers never did rise to overthrow the Weimar Republic established after World War I.

Lenin and the Bolsheviks held onto the power they had seized. It became evident that the German workers, divided into the rival Socialist and Communist parties, would not follow Lenin's lead. Consequently, the Bolsheviks settled down to rule Russia and to build it industrially as a wholly-owned state enterprise.

The important point, however, is that the Soviet Union during its entire existence was a huge laboratory testing what happens when private property, apart from personal possessions like clothing, is abolished. If Marx was right about private property and its influence, then what would happen would be the development of a society bathed in benignity and kindliness of man toward man. But the actuality is that the Soviet Union became a society unparalleled in all history for mass cruelty to its own people, most of them lowly working people. What happened was that the state became the only employer and anyone seeking a better personal life and higher earnings had to please his employer. And if that employer required, as the Soviet Union did, that people be constantly harried, spied upon and arrested for the slightest infractions, ambitious employees had to satisfy the demands of the state.

Those ambitious employees sought the most prestigious bureaucratic jobs, becoming what were known as *apparatchniks*. As the salaries of these individuals were set at the same level as those of the workers in accord with socialist doctrine, they obtained their special privileges through a system that allowed them to purchase all manner of goods at deep discounts in secret stores, to have the use of commodious apartments, automobiles and country houses at absurdly low prices and to enjoy travel and resort privileges, all at very low discounted prices. This level of people lived like affluent capitalists while the nation as a whole groaned under constant torture and deprivation. Those of this privileged class were known as members of the *nomenklatura* or "named ones."

Actually, contrary to Marx, private property, if the ownership is widely spread, has a stabilizing effect in society. It produces tranquility rather than hardship. People don't need private property to be provoked to show their selfish sides. Those sides are natural, inherent, as these pages show.

Marx got his idea of the cruelty of capitalism from British parliamentary reports of investigations in the early 19th century of conditions in British factories and mines. They were horrendous. Women and children worked long hours for pittances, half naked, in mines and manufacturing establishments. But all this, bad as it was, was a tea party compared with the han-

dling of people later in the Soviet Union. The mere
fact of a parliamentary investigation that turned in
critical reports contrasted with Soviet indifference to
the condition of workers.

What happened under early English capitalism is
what happens to any phase of enterprise, anywhere,
that is unregulated. And in the Soviet Union there
was no protective regulation or official criticism of
what went on.

After Lenin's death in 1924 the Communist Party
was ruled by its Central Committee and its politburo
but in the mid-1930s all the previous leaders were executed by Stalin on fabricated charges after a series of
purely ceremonial trials. The effects of these party
purges extended down through the ranks of the party.
They left Stalin in sole command of the state apparatus. The wrath of the secret police apparatus was now
turned on all party members except those loyal to
Stalin.

Both Stalin and Lenin were criminals by every
standard of western law long before the Bolshevik
revolution and both had spent time in Czarist prisons. Lenin was especially fond of Stalin because the
latter was the chief money-raiser of the party by
means of armed bank robberies he directed and in
which he participated. For the Bolshevik wing of the
Social Democratic Party could not have existed on the
basis of the meager dues it collected from its few
members. In order to support its publications and its
network of agents abroad, money was needed and

was supplied through bank robberies. As Lenin put it, they robbed the robbers.

As in all social combat organizations it was first necessary to demonize the opponents, the capitalists. This was done very thoroughly by Marx and the Marxists, who held them responsible for all social ills. Essentially the same thing was done later by Hitler only now it was Socialists, Jews and Communists who were demonized. Those whom all revolutionaries wish to destroy they first demonize.

It was the claim of the totalitarians that by concentrating authority as they did, they were able to get things done expeditiously. This was true. But it was also true that the concentration of authority prevented timely or rational action. By way of illustration consider Stalin's refusal to heed warnings rained in upon him by his own intelligence agents that Hitler planned to attack the Soviet Union in 1941. No amount of evidence could convince Stalin. The consequence was that no precautions were taken to move vulnerable equipment such as airplanes from easy access by an attacker.

The reason Stalin did not bestir himself was that he erroneously saw Hitler as a careful calculator like himself. Why then should Hitler attack? He was obtaining all he wanted to in the way of raw materials and other supplies from the Soviet Union under the Soviet-Nazi treaty and since the fall of France, Hitler was the master of Europe from Gibraltar to the North Cape and the Atlantic Ocean to the Soviet

Union. The German dictator ruled over more of Europe than anyone ever had. Therefore, Stalin felt secure against Hitler. But he was wrong.

Hitler, in deciding to invade the Soviet Union on June 22, 1941, overruled his own General Staff. These highly trained officers advised against tackling the Soviet Union with its vast distances and enormous resources. But Hitler, the one-time army corporal, felt that his intuition was flawless. For wasn't it he who had overrun Poland and annexed Czechoslovakia and Austria and captured all of France against the advice of experts from the very beginning. He had even been advised against invading the Rhineland, his first daring move.

Hitler's early successes came about in part because his chosen enemies believed nobody would be so foolish as to try anything like that. They were therefore not braced for his early onslaughts, hadn't had a chance to show their mettle or even mobilize their thoughts.

Nineteen forty-one was the year when Hitler's run of luck ended. For in addition to launching his invasion of the Soviet Union in June, he also joined with Tojo of Japan in December in declaring war on the United States, his worst error of all. Furthermore, in the invasion of the Soviet Union, he again ignored his generals and split his forces three ways—toward Leningrad, Moscow and the oil fields of Baku. What he should have done was concentrate all his forces on taking Moscow before winter set in, then turn to Leningrad and finally go after the oil fields.

But Hitler needed oil immediately for his large forces, oil that had previously been flowing to him from Stalin. His right wing, bound for the oil fields, was stalled at Stalingrad where it was ultimately annihilated.

The Soviet generals, meanwhile, allowed Hitler to extend his forces as far as possible without achieving their ultimate aim and then in a classic military move they counter-attacked in force up the center and didn't stop driving until the Russian army reached Berlin in 1945.

Furthermore, with the Russians now pounding his forces unmercifully, Hitler had brought the United States into the fray. Had Hitler not declared war on the United States, the United States would never have entered World War II. For the anti-war movement in the United States, despite sympathy for Britain and France, was overwhelmingly strong, owing to many years of disclosures about deceit, chicanery, profiteering and disappointment with respect to World War I. Wilson's policies were wholly discredited and large meetings of an organization called America First were held all over the country, addressed by eminent personages including folk hero Colonel Charles A. Lindbergh.

At the time, these America Firsters were contemptuously called isolationists by pro-Allied interventionists. The latter were apparently not aware that

George Washington was the first American isolationist and every American president since his time until Wilson had followed in Washington's footsteps. It was Wilson's massive interventionist blunder in 1914-18 that made the United States a party to the European devil's cauldron.

The triumph of the isolationists in keeping the United States out of the war was abruptly ended on December 7, 1941, when the Japanese bombed Pearl Harbor and sank almost the entire Pacific fleet. The Japanese action had nothing to do with Hitler's enterprise in Europe but he allied himself with it by declaring war on the United States.

The Japanese attacked at Pearl Harbor because the United States, not relishing Japan's continued assault on China, had threatened to cut off Japan's oil supplies coming north from Indonesia. The sinking of the American fleet made such action against Japan impossible for the moment and the Japanese hoped that ultimately they could achieve a negotiated peace with the United States.

Japan was badly beaten by the United States before the two atomic bombs were dropped. Most of its navy and merchant shipping had been sunk and conventional bombing had destroyed half of Tokyo. The Japanese high command was as poor a calculator as was Hitler.

However, Japan's assault on Pearl Harbor was, from the point of view of Japanese strategy, a defensive move. Here it should be noted that in modern war, there is properly no such thing as defense in the sense of repelling an attack.

This fact was unquestionably known to the New Dealers in Washington when they cynically changed the name of the War Department to the Defense Department. The change was made for strictly propaganda purposes to lull a gullible public into believing they were being made safe from attack. The same psychology had led the French government to build the Maginot Line, an ineffectual fortification. They should have heeded the dictum of their own Marshal Ferdinand Foch, who said the best defense is attack. The Japanese were certainly convinced of this prior to Pearl Harbor, for which they were berated as dastardly sneaks by President Roosevelt who called it "a day that will live in infamy."

There is absolutely no defense in modern warfare, a fact that was recognized during the Soviet-American rivalry in building nuclear bombs and the missiles to deliver them. Where the two nations were heading before the Soviet Union collapsed under the weight of its own ineptitude was toward nuclear warfare in which one-third to one-half of the American population would be destroyed and the Soviet population would have been virtually annihilated. That day of horrendous reckoning has at least been postponed.

The Japanese finally recognized that they had no defense when they abruptly capitulated after the atomic bombings of Hiroshima and Nagasaki.

There being no defense, the name of Defense Department should be abolished by the United States and the old honest name of War Department restored.

In addition to the erroneous thinking about defense there is also error in references to fighting in modern war. For there is little action properly describable as fighting in modern warfare. The so-called combatants in modern war are really mechanics who operate lethal machines: revolvers, automatic pistols, machine guns, breech-loading repeating rifles and rockets (all of which, incidentally, were invented by Americans, who also invented the submarine, the airplane and the atomic bomb).

The Turks, of course, get the credit for inventing genocide although the Germans put it on an efficient mechanical basis as well as inventing poison gas for warfare. To the British goes credit for inventing the armored truck and radar although Americans long ago invented the armored battleship. The Germans invented the long range cannon—Big Bertha—but also more significantly improved the rocket so that it became satisfactorily lethal.

One can't think of much that the Japanese or the French contributed to modern war although to the Chinese goes the great credit for the invention of gunpowder. A Swede, Alfred Nobel, invented dynamite so the Swedes cannot be denied honor for destructiveness.

But Americans living in the United States did the most to develop modern armaments. The reason for this is that Americans are a bellicose people although they are repeatedly hailed in their own newspapers and by their politicians as notably peace-loving. Nothing could be further from the truth, probably because they have been continually fighting for some 300 years to subdue the continent. First they fought the French, then the British, Spanish and Mexicans and all the while they kept up a running combat against the native aborigines.

Guns were also freely employed in killing wild animals, most of whom were wantonly destroyed in a display of superfluous marksmanship. Unquestionably more harmless animals have been destroyed in a short period of time on the North American continent than anywhere else on earth.

So that is where we are, in a world where "peace-loving" refers to those who are war-like. Propaganda not only exaggerates but completely reverses meanings. Political propaganda particularly softens the rough edges of language by introducing euphemisms. For example, the worst thing that can happen to a bank is to shut down; so when the New Dealers shut down all banks for several days in the 1930s they called it a "bank holiday." The banks at the time were in serious trouble and had to be bailed out by the government. A holiday, of course, is a time of jollification and celebration, which the government's use of language invited everyone to participate in. It was like treating a death in the family as a fortunate event.

In the same way the government changed the name of conscription, which forces men into the armed forces, to "selective service," suggesting that those who were called upon to face death on the battlefield had been picked from among many for some distinguished work. "Tax increase" to the politicians is made into "revenue enhancement," a presumably desirable turn of events. And so it goes; to the propagandist white is black and black is white. Anything to keep the victims happy as they are being led to the slaughter.

More recently, in the Balkans, the term "ethnic cleansing" has been shown to mean the mass extermination of helpless people, including women, children and the aged. The "ethnic cleansing" also included the rape of thousands of Bosnian women by Serbs. Each one of three or four ethnic groups in the region has taken turns over the generations at killing and torturing the others, leaving a legacy of hatred and group feuds.

Enough has been written here about the role of governments in all the world destruction to give the reader some idea of what has been happening. Readers can obtain more details about the horror story by consulting the rubrics of "totalitarianism and the World Wars" in their public libraries. Hundreds of books have been written on these subjects. But even reading the many books will not adequately present the full story of man's faithlessness to his own avowed high principles.

The situation is essentially the same, at all times, in Africa and Latin America, where there is always armed warfare and internal insurrection taking place between nations or tribes. The entire human race, more or less, is catering to self-interest at the expense of the general interest, with governments often participating in the deviation.

Here and there, explorers find in distant jungles, isolated tribes that are described as especially gentle and peaceful, giving color to Rousseau's vision of the noble savage. But there is no way of checking on these reports and, even if they are true, they are but details in a massive history of rapine, looting and wholesale destruction in most of the world.

The Internal Guerilla War of Crime

In all countries throughout the world there is being carried on at all times a running guerilla warfare against the population, contrary to the rules of justice and equity nominally defended by the governments. This guerilla warfare, largely individualistic but also carried on by gangs, is commonly called crime.

There has been crime in all periods of history but now, in the wake of two World Wars, the Korean War, the Vietnam war and a variety of other localized wars, it is especially great, as though people have been inspired by the violence of the governments in general. There is more crime in some countries than in others, for special reasons. In the United States the tide of crime has been steadily rising through the years and is

now at a very high level. Since the breakup of the Soviet Union, individual crime in its regions has greatly
increased. Wherever one looks there is crime, either a
great deal or at least some. In some parts of the world,
such as Scandinavia and Switzerland, it seems relatively
little but in other parts such as Italy and the United
States, it is very great. In all the largest countries such
as Germany, France and Great Britain it is a problem.

A cross-sectional view of crime in the United States
is given in the following data taken from "Crime in
the United States of America," 1991 *Uniform Crime
Reports*, Federal Bureau of Investigation:

Violent Crimes, 1991................................1,911,770
Property Crimes, 1991..........................12,961,100
Murder and homicide 24,700
Forcible rape...106,590
Robbery 687,730
Burglary 3,157,290
Larceny theft..8,142,200

The rate of crimes per 100,000 of population was
5,897.8 crimes. Violent crimes had increased by 33.7
percent since 1981.

According to the *National Crime Victimization
Survey* of the United States Department of Justice 24
percent of American households were victimized by
crime in each of the years 1990 and 1991. This figure
sustains the view that there is an unorganized guerilla
war taking place.

In 1991 prison population in the United States was 823,414, a record. Of these, according to the Department of Justice, the total sentenced to more than one year was 789,261.

In 1991, 69 police officers were feloniously slain, four more than in 1990; and 52 officers were killed in accidents while on duty. According to the FBI Reports for 1991, law enforcement agencies of the country had 3.1 persons on their staffs per 1,000 of population. This police personnel was distributed among 12,805 local, state and federal police agencies. Private police hired by big business and institutions exceeded this number.

Police directly prevent very little crime, contrary to popular supposition. Deterrence of criminals by the police comes about through their capture of suspected criminals, an object lesson for all observers. Whatever deterrence there is by the court system stems from the trial and conviction of offenders—another object lesson for observers. The presumption of law enforcement people is that capture, trial and conviction of criminals will deter other people from violating the law.

Unfortunately in the United States there is a large public constituency that sentimentally favors criminals rather than victims of crime. These people feel the criminal was driven to commit the crime by the hard conditions of his upbringing, his inability to hold on to a job and his consequent poverty.

Sympathy for the criminal extends to murderers so

that in some states there is no death penalty for murder. And as a result of this sentimental constituency many convicts are quickly paroled and upon release commit more crimes. The average time served in prison for murder in the United States is now seven years! The prisons are overcrowded and in many states the voters refuse to endorse the building of more prisons owing to what the cost would be in new taxes. This is especially true in Florida.

One reason for the public sympathy with criminals, even murderers, is that the public sees them sitting in court like trapped animals. The public does not see their many victims. As for dead victims the public feels they cannot be restored to life and therefore should be forgotten. Because of this, those who favor the criminal subtly focus attention away from thoughts of the victims.

It is argued that the death penalty does not deter. Indeed, nothing whatever deters criminals absolutely. But the experience of governments has long been that the quick application of punishment to all miscreants is the best known instrument of deterrence. In totalitarian countries governments were able to even silence all criticism of government.

Apparently in the United States the tide of crime will have to rise to still higher levels before sufficient public pressure is induced to produce more onerous punishments. For as matters now stand there is in the United States widespread contempt for the law, often shown even by ordinarily law-abiding people.

Hume's formulation of the problem of human behavior is most directly applicable to the commission
of individual crime. Hume, in his day, did not note
that government can be taken over by obvious criminals like the totalitarians and used as their tool. Nor
did he note that even an elected government can be
corrupted into catering to powerful special interests,
to the sacrifice of justice and equity. Government, in
brief, can be misused to criminal ends.

As we have seen in two World Wars and many localized wars, government is capable of completely
nullifying the rules of justice and equity. In the wrong
hands or devoted to the wrong interests it is the great
destroyer of modern times, more so than any plague.

On the other hand, in its normal peace-time role it
is, as Hume pointed out, man's guide upward from
the lowest pits to the heights of civilization. It is the
creator of schools, libraries, parks, hospitals and scientific laboratories, the crude regulator of affairs
throughout society. Unfortunately, when it elects to
go into combat under modern conditions and with
modern technical means of destruction, it threatens to
undo everything that has been slowly achieved over
scores of generations. Like a frenzied gambler, it can
lose its entire substance in a single venture or can
completely destroy itself as did the government of the
Russian czar, the Hapsburg government of Austria-
Hungary, the Turkish sultanate and others in a long
historical procession.

Disrespect for law in the United States derives from

the sentimental approach to punishment of all kinds. Not only is the death penalty excluded in some state jurisdictions but parole is freely used to release dangerous multiple offenders from prison. Manifestly, parole should be abolished entirely. As to the influence of punishment on careless members of the populace, one recalls the story of the man who was beating his mule over the head with a club. A bystander objected to such cruelty to which the mule's owner replied: "I'm just trying to get his attention."

More than light sentences are required to engage the attention of most law-breakers, and more than imprisonment for murder. As to the claimed failure of the death penalty to deter murderers, all experience shows the precise opposite. It is sometimes argued that when a death penalty is carried out and the prisoner is in fact innocent there is no way of redressing the injustice. But the way to avoid this injustice is to be sure the evidence sustains the conviction.

It happens that police and prosecutors sometimes obtain a conviction by means of manufactured evidence or by withholding exculpatory evidence. Police and prosecutors do this in order to convince their constituents they are more efficient than they really are in solving crimes, an instance of moral depravity on the individual level in government. The way to avoid this sort of contretemps is to scrutinize with special care the evidence on which anyone is convicted. The slightest deficiency in the evidence would be a reason for requiring a new trial or a dismissal of the charge.

Some people are imprisoned for long terms on the basis of faulty evidence, a serious miscarriage of justice. The new procedures of DNA testing have shown several cases in which convicted persons were indubitably innocent. But the mere fact that someone may be erroneously convicted, an event that occasionally occurs, is no reason for doing away with punishment entirely.

However, it is no use arguing with those who favor leniency toward people convicted of crimes, for they are adamant. The remedy for this situation will have to come from rising public consciousness as the toll of crime increases, as it is surely doing under the policy of leniency.

It is the sentimental concept of leniency that encourages the widespread contempt for law in the United States, at every level of society. As any reader can see, I am a hard-liner in support of respect for established law.

Special reasons why there is so much crime in the United States are the following:

The United States is not only very large but it is also very loosely organized under the Constitution, giving it a cluster of fifty state governments under a federal government and more than 3,000 counties as well as hundreds of municipalities. One part of this melange often does not know what is happening in another part. Mix into this complicated structure a polyglot population many of whom are illegal immigrants or recent legal immigrants. This is not to say that recent immigrants, legal or illegal, themselves commit crimes but they do tend to destabilize the established population in the competition for low-paying jobs so that many of the younger people turn to crime for a livelihood, specializing more particularly in the sale of illegal drugs.

Additionally, the United States contains segments of population that are alienated and will not perform according to established standards. The earliest of these segments were the aborigines or American Indians, who simply refused to take up the ways of the white man. Others are uneducated blacks who were little noticed as long as they were share-croppers in the South but who have more recently, owing to the mechanization of agriculture, been pushed on to the cities. These uneducated, poorly reared young blacks commit a very large proportion of the street crimes and occupy a disproportionate amount of prison space.

On top of all this there is the large sentimental strata of white population that believes people are forced into a life of crime by the harshness of their upbringing or their deprived condition. As to this, it should be noticed that no condition whatever forces people to commit any crime. Most poor people do not commit any crime. Indeed, most monstrous crimes are committed by people who are not poor but who are middle or upper class. The most lucrative and sweeping crimes of all are committed by corporations, whose officers and directors are rarely sent to prison. The records of the Department of Justice contain the names of hundreds of corporations that have been convicted and more or less moderately fined.

Crime has no necessary or invariable connection with poverty, poor upbringing or lack of education, although people reared in these circumstances may be included among criminals. And many serious crimes such as murder, rape, and assault have no discernible economic or financial motivation attached to them. People may commit crimes simply out of irrational hostility or ill will.

But the possibility of evading or reducing punishment for the commission of crime in the United States is what undoubtedly encourages the commission of much crime. The criminal usually feels there is a good chance he will go free or serve a greatly reduced prison term.

If, without bringing forward any complicated plans for the reform and regeneration of society, people only obeyed existing laws, the world would suddenly become a much better place for everybody to live in. What adds to the natural dangers of the world is man-made danger, which in the ordinary course of events is much more threatening than any natural danger. If people merely obeyed the traffic laws, did not exceed the legal speed limits or drive through red lights, thousands of lives would be saved each year. But people will not comply with the laws at the cost of their own convenience. In consequence, government in its law-enforcing phase of operations, only does the best it can. And this often isn't enough.

It is clear, then, that it is people in the mass, going their individual separate ways in pursuit of their individual near term interests, who cause the most trouble in the world. But even in this prospect there is material for the hardy optimist who thinks along the lines of Bernard de Mandeville's *The Fable of the Bees*, an eighteenth-century literary classic whose thesis is that private vices confer public benefits. In the case of crime the benefits are the remunerative work it gives to lawyers, judges, bailiffs, court clerks, prosecutors, police, prison wardens and guards.

To this list may be added psychiatrists, social workers and statisticians. Similarly, the spinoff of benefits from war are the employment of munitions and transport workers and the work provided for surgeons, nurses and workers in veterans' hospitals.

To this may be added employment for all the burial parties, cemetery keepers and construction workers who are ultimately called upon to repair the damage. The rebuilding of Germany and Japan provided many jobs. Simple activity of any kind, constructive or destructive, yields some kind of remunerative employment for somebody.

Government and Religion

Down through the ages, governments have sought the aid and support of religions in enforcing the rules of justice and equity. The Emperor Constantine I (280-337 A.D.) even made Christianity mandatory for Roman citizens in order to shore up his disintegrating empire.

The aim of governments in seeking the support of religions and religious people has been to transfer fear of violating God's ordinances into fear of violating mundane governmental ordinances. Most religions endorse support of the secular laws. When a religion does not do so, it is an adversary of the established government.

The value to government of bringing in religion is to enlist the fear of disobeying God's ordinances on the side of support for the secular laws, which often themselves seek support from God. A residue of this religious entanglement with government in the American system is the Biblical oath still administered in courts and the Biblical oath of office taken by elected officials up to the president. While one may refuse to take this oath, to do so places one under suspicion by millions of religious people.

Every religion without exception consists of an elementary moral code, such as the Ten Commandments and the rules of organization for that religion. All of this is encased in some preposterous myth, such as the life and death of Jesus, or Moses coming down from the mountain with stone slabs on which were engraved the Ten Commandments. Other religions are supported by other myths and some religions, such as Hinduism, are ruled over by many gods.

Whenever religionists argue the superior validity of their religion over other religions, they are really arguing the superior validity of one myth over the other, a patent absurdity as no myth whatever has objective validity. Every myth is a product of human imagination and wishful thinking. And wishful thinking is a hallmark of every religion.

But as history shows, organized religions like governments often come into conflict and bring about the violent deaths of thousands of people, even millions. When religions do come into violent conflict, or sects within a single religion conflict, the conflict is always about the acquisition or retention of members, who are the customers of any religion. Governments fight over territories and the populations therein and religions fight over members.

Often it is difficult to distinguish a religious war from a political war, as in the Christian crusades against Islam which left Islam shattered even though it embodied a higher intellectual level at the time than did Christianity. It was not until after the Renaissance that Christianity gradually shook off the most retrograde of its teachings.

After the wars of the crusades, Christianity split into its Catholic and Protestant divisions and conducted fearful and bloody wars against each other for many years in Europe. Residual wars of these religious wars are still going on during this writing such as the case of the Orthodox Serbs against the Muslim Bosnians, with the struggle taking place over territory and population. At this writing thousands of unarmed Bosnian civilians have been killed or raped. In India, Hindus and Muslims are waging pitched battles against each other, with much loss of life.

Although the Biblical oath is freely taken in courts, it does not deter lawyers from conducting severe and highly skeptical cross-examinations, often showing that witnesses have been boldly lying or grossly mistaken. Ten people can testify that someone was present at the commission of a crime but if it can be shown that that person was at that moment at some official conference 100 miles away, the oath-sworn testimony of the ten is nullified.

An oath makes nothing certain, not even an intention. Lawyers know that witnesses in court frequently lie or are ludicrously mistaken.

In science no oath whatever is valid. A scientist who offered to take an oath certifying to the truth of some finding would be the subject of scorn. In science every claim to an experimental result or the truth of some observation is subjected to validation by other scientists. If the experiment or the observation cannot be repeated the original claim is discharged as unscientific and deemed untrue. An oath in science is a superfluous joke, showing that the unsupported claims of people, no matter how sincere, are not to be trusted. Or trusted only at one's peril.

Despite the invalidity of religion, many non-religious conservatives nevertheless believe religion does serve as a deterrence to misbehavior. And so it probably does, in a certain number of cases. But it is plainly evident in multitudes of criminal cases that crimes have been committed by people claiming to be religious. Here a distinction is to be drawn between the truly religious person and the nominally religious. The truly religious person will not commit a crime but the nominally religious will. Unfortunately, one cannot tell the difference by mere observation between the nominally and the truly religious.

Not only do members of religious organizations commit crimes but clergy often do—crimes such as sexual molestation of children, rape, adultery, embezzlement of church funds and the like. The Holy Ghost appears to have been impotent in keeping these people in the ranks of rectitude, much to the dismay of conservative supporters of religion. The conservatives, however, have a point on their side that some religious people are law-abiding. But so are some non-religious people.

It is clear, at any rate, that religion has no particular influence in inducing the support of law. This is proven by the fact that the prisons are full of people who were reared under religious auspices.

Interlude of Review

The argument is that mankind is bound by innate temperament to prefer the near-term gratification of his desires at the sacrifice of his long-term interests. This has been demonstrated through the ages since the first emergence of civilization. These interests have been collectively and serially articulated in public by succeeding generations and are publicly endorsed by most rational men but they are constantly being nullified by anarchic individual action. It is the same as though individual players on a team refuse to play by the established rules or prefer to deviate from them *ad libidtum.*

The philosopher David Hume saw all this taking place in daily society under an established government and he saw all the rules as being the products of serial government action down through the centuries. He did not, however, visualize that the men in charge of governments would from time to time violate the rules of their own governnment or that men in the course of time would replace their traditional governments with eccentric totalitarian governments that impose separate totalitarian rules superseding all established rules of justice and equity.

Justice consists in confirming and defending whatever any individual naturally possesses: life, physical safety, liberty, property, the operative use of all his senses and faculties such as speaking, reading, writing, moving about in public places and peacefully associating with other people. Totalitarian and autocratic governments, under the pretext of improving conditions, first impede liberty by prohibiting free movement, then under the code of censorship prohibit free speech and communication and finally require that everybody obtain governmental permission to travel about.

Under free government people are permitted to select employment within their capabilities and available opportunities. Under totalitarianism people are assigned to jobs. In a free society people are permitted to participate in making their own rules of governance; in a totalitarian society all such rules are handed down by a remote government, by a politburo or a central committee.

The results of a free government are not a heaven on earth, by any means. Far from it. But as the experience of the twentieth century shows the results of a free society are always better by far than those of a closed society, no matter how many loose ends and imperfections remain.

Social critics may perform a valuable role when they point out defects in the existing society and government, as when they criticized the institution of slavery. But they clearly go too far when they advocate the scuttling of an existing free government and prescribe its replacement by a hypothetically better government such as the socialists have done. While the expressed aims of socialism may be admirable there is no evidence whatever that those aims could be attained by the means advocated. And enforced totalitarian socialism, such as Lenin and the Bolsheviks sponsored, will certainly fail under any circumstances.

Force may accomplish many things but it cannot make a people productive and creative. No amount of force can make a scholar out of a dunce, no matter how hard the dunce strives to comply with the mandates of his masters.

Governments Against Each Other

Governments are all in a "state of nature" vis-a-vis each other. That is to say, there is no set of rules with an enforcement mechanism to regulate the relations of one government with the others. Each government legally has what is called sovereignty or supreme power.

The principal result of this situation is that when disputes arise and cannot be resolved by negotiation there is resort to force by each of the parties—that is, there is war.

While there is such a thing as international law, consisting of agreed upon terms of intercourse among governments, there is no way of enforcing these laws other than by armed conflict among the parties.

As to Europe and nations derived from Europe it may be pointed out that all more or less officially subscribe to Christianity and should be able to settle disputes according to the tenets of this religion. But nothing so clearly reveals the futility of religion as a regulating mechanism than the religions prevailing among nations.

The nations of Europe that became involved in World War I had monarchs who were either the heads of the national Christian church or had high official status in it as did the emperors of Austria-Hungary, Russia and Germany. The king of Great Britain was the head of the Church of England. As far as the governments of all the belligerents were concerned, the role of religion was principally that of manipulating each populace in support of the government.

As for taking the religion seriously in its precepts all these governments in effect thumbed their noses at it.

With each government standing above all acceptable rules of conduct or international law and not even responsive to the precepts of the religion it professed, they were all back in a state of nature like a pack of snarling savages except that these governmental savages were armed with highly destructive weapons.

They already had before them an example of what such weapons, not yet fully developed, could do in the case of the American civil war of 1861-65, but they chose to ignore this sanguinary lesson or were simply ignorant of it.

Governments, in other words, make their own rules, like jungle animals, and are willing, as two world wars show, to push their authority to the maximum. World War II did not end until one side faced virtual annihilation by the Bomb.

Possessed of so much power, the leaders of governments come to feel they are invincible and embark on hare-brained adventures like the Vietnam war, carried on at great distances against a jungle-screened foe that could have been destroyed had full power been brought against it. But to have brought full power against such a puny foe would have made the United States a pariah among nations.

Yet, until the collapse of the Soviet Union, the United States and the Soviet Union were on a collision course that promised colossal disaster for both.

Admittedly there are religious rules, the rules of Christianity, to govern the behavior of nations. But these rules, with their promise of divine punishment, are even more remote from the perception of governments than the rules of government are from the perception of the common man. And the divine rules are not implemented with immediate enforcement and punishment as are the governmental rules regulating its citizens. Nobody goes to jail or is executed for disobeying the divine rules that virtually all politicians mindlessly extol at every opportunity.

We see, then, that government plays a dual role in the world. It imposes, more or less effectively, the rules of justice and equity on its own populace but in a Jekyll-Hyde turnabout it can become crazily destructive in trying to impose its will on another government. Moreover, governments easily overestimate the extent of their power as did both Austria-Hungary and Czarist Russia in 1914. The ministers of such paper sovereignties are taken in by their own marching bands, flying flags and cheering crowds.

Governments, in short, are interchangeably good and bad. Even when they are good during any peacetime they may not be perfect. But whatever there is of justice and equity in the world is attributable to free governments.

Without being bolstered by government, mankind simply slips into a state of sodden savagery on an individual basis. The elements always trying to lead the way into such savagery are the deliberately criminal elements at all levels of society. But if such elements gain ascendancy, everybody else must join them in the same game if only as a matter of self defense. Then everybody is on the same destructive footing.

The Corruption of Governments

Hume was aware that even a free republican government can be corrupted, to a greater or lesser extent. As he wrote in his essay, cited above, "It is a necessary precaution in a free state to change the governors frequently, which obliges these temporary tyrants to be more expeditious and rapacious, that they may accumulate sufficient wealth before they give place to their successors." But it is necessary that the government be so constituted that it is able nevertheless to carry out its major constructive roles.

Corruption in a free republican government can injure its standing in the public eye and can diminish its effectiveness, but such a government must be able to transcend the corruption and uproot it.

While corruption is experienced in different instances and times in all republican governments, it is usually not as widespread as that disclosed in Italy beginning in 1992. There, as it turned out, leading figures of all parties were involved for years in the grossest sort of corruption: the taking of bribes in return for the placing of government contracts with private corporations. High officials were shown to be in close contact with the Mafia.

As a consequence of these disclosures, public confidence in the Italian government became very low and disgust with it quite general but the broad work of the government nevertheless continued. Kindergartens and schools still functioned, libraries remained open, streets and neighborhoods remained orderly as if out of habit, museums and private enterprises still functioned. Meanwhile a large group of high public officials was discredited and put under investigation and prepared for trial.

Every republican government has experienced something of the same sort. Since its beginning the United States has experienced a series of corruption scandals on the federal, state and municipal levels. Yet, despite the scandals, the government, whether federal or local, continued to function in its broad outlines in sustaining the populace.

Corruption, of course, entails an additional heavy expense laid both directly and indirectly on the populace. And those who are disclosed as corrupt remain in public disgrace even after serving sentences in jail. The punishment awaiting the corrupt does not seem to deter ventures in corruption, showing that government officials often have the same dim apprehension of the proper rules of lawful conduct as does the general public.

But prosecutors, police and partisan critics of corruption have a vivid sense of those rules and through public clamor proceed to impress them on the public mind. Only if the government is poorly constructed, as in the case of many South American republics, does the corruption seem to eventuate in a total collapse of the government usually followed by a military dictatorship.

The sort of corruption sporadically disclosed in a government like that of the United States reminds one very much of a prized dog that is infested with fleas. The dog more or less continuously scratches at the fleas to get rid of them but never quite succeeds. Corruption is apparently something that can never be completely eliminated from government because too often public officials have as dim an apprehension of the rules as do common criminals.

President Richard Nixon as a trained lawyer certainly knew he was breaking the rules of government right and left but he was too intent on pursuing his own political feuds to heed them. Flea-infested dogs are subjected to flea-baths to get rid of all the invaders at a stroke. There is, however, no such general cleansing process for government. There the invading fleas must be detected and eliminated one by one, a tedius, painstaking and more or less perpetual process.

Innocent Law Abiding People

It is not to be denied that, relatively speaking, there are such. However, everybody harbors to some extent the weakness of allowing some of his individual projects to proceed in defiance of the collective rules meant to protect each individual from harm. The rule-breaker ignores these rules and in the process injures someone somewhere.

As there are no statistics covering those people who adhere with some fidelity to the rules laid down by governments, the best one can do is rely on direct personal observation. It is my belief that the following groups of people strongly tend to abide by the rules of society although here and there some individuals may deviate: librarians, nurses, teachers, judges and prosecutors.

Judging by reports in the press, the same cannot be said of other large groups of people such as businessmen, lawyers, politicians and, in general, everybody who is intimately concerned with handling other people's money or property. And as to popular lore about lawyers, it is a fact that some lawyers are almost obsessively devoted to observing the laws. I have known some.

Just about everybody who deals with money and property is under constant temptation to employ what is popularly known as "sticky fingers"—that is, to help themselves surreptitiously.

The constant strong temptation such people are under shows the necessity for the existence of government with its remedial laws.

The Need for Strict Laws

Considering the ease with which many people lose sight of the need for observing the laws, it is necessary for governments to have strict laws, strictly enforced. These are needed as a forceful reminder of the laws.

Contemporary thinking, however, appears to be moving in a contrary direction, a mistake. Public sympathy, at least in the United States, seems to be engaged with the criminal who has been caught and faces a long prison term or execution and to be unaware of the less visible victims of the crime, who may be suffering excruciatingly. Here is another case where the nearer and more visible phenomenon appears to affect the minds of observers more vividly than the distant crime.

Government has no way except by forceful reminder to make people seriously aware of the law—by fines, imprisonment and execution. For many people don't get the point by a mere publication of the laws. However, when laws are leniently enforced, as in the United States, persons disposed to break the laws come, more or less, to feel contempt both for the government and its laws. The general consequence is a rising crime curve, such as we see in the United States.

And to the contention that punishment like a death penalty does not deter, one can examine the entire crime picture and see that nothing whatever deters absolutely. For many who commit crimes despite the laws are gambling that they will be lucky and not caught or, if caught, not convicted thanks to the good offices of some clever lawyer.

Another reason for lenient sentences and early parole that appeals to a section of the public is that both reduce prison costs. There is, too, a constituency that is opposed to building more prisons because of the cost in new taxes. Those who take this attitude place their purses above the safety of themselves and their neighbors.

For present-day criminals are often ruthless, as the bombing of the World Trade Center in New York early in 1993 demonstrated. It is easy to see that those who placed this bomb would have preferred to have placed an atomic bomb that would have devastated the region for thirty miles or so around. As far as that goes, one deliberate felonious killing has as much venom behind it as the killing of a million.

A more general reason for seeking leniency for criminals is the anarchistic belief that all people are basically good and have been corrupted by government down through the ages. Hence the anarchist desire to abolish government and let the good times roll. All history clamors against that notion, which anarchists and extreme libertarians nevertheless cling to as an article of faith. It so happens, for whatever it may be worth, that Christianity agrees with Hume that all men are sinners—or worse. So Hume's view is not as bizarre as anarchists would suppose.

The Unfair State

Although it is the state that is the source of whatever justice and equity there is in the world, the state, and more particularly the elective state, is far from perfect in its deliverances, as anyone can see.

Politicians and news media people seem agreed that any elective government is also a "democratic" government. Thus the Nicaraguan government that succeeded the Soviet-sponsored Sandinistas is referred to as a democratic government. Any elected government is so designated, apparently because such a designation is flattering to the electorate, which mistakenly believes it is running the government.

As a matter of fact, under no government in the entire world does the populace have anything *directly* to say about shaping government policy. Under the United States Constitution, people vote for candidates who have fixed terms. Winners in an election may or may not perform as they have promised voters. If the voters do not approve of their performance they may refuse to re-elect them when their terms have expired. The writers of the U.S. Constitution called this republican government. They were strongly opposed to democratic government, as anyone can discover by reading Madison's Notes on the convention of 1787. Democracy to the American founders was simple nonsense.

The way the idea of democracy became prevalent in American thinking was through the founding of the Republican-Democratic Party by Thomas Jefferson as the vehicle for his election as president in 1800. In 1828 the Jacksonians, finding the word "democratic" more popular, changed the name to the Democratic Party, which quickly fell under the control of the Southern slaveocracy. It became the nurturing ground of the civil war on the basis of Jefferson's divisive principle of "states rights" laid down originally in the Virginia and Kentucky Resolutions. The leaders of this party became the leaders of the Confederacy in the bloody Civil War.

These same people opposed the addition of the 13th, 14th and 15th amendments to the Constitution, after the Civil War. They were associated with the Ku Klux Klan and in the 1870s came to a rapprochement

with the newly-born Republican Party to apply Jim
Crow treatment to newly-freed blacks, thereby keeping them in a state of quasi-servitude or helotry for
nearly ten decades.

This policy was reinforced in 1896 with the *Plessy
vs. Ferguson* decision of the Supreme Court. This decision allowed "separate but equal" facilities for
blacks.

Just how democratic any of this was is more than
questionable.

In a final salute to the Old South, Secretary of the
Navy Josephus Daniels in the Democratic Wilson
Administration of 1912-1920 ordered all Negroes in
the Navy to serve only as cooks, busboys and waiters.
Until then blacks had served commendably as en-
listed men of all grades in the Republican-run Navy.
Was this action in any way democratic? Or even de-
cent?

The Republican Party, upon making its peace with
the Democratic Party, was brought under the control
of the northern industrialists and financiers.

In sum, one major party was first under the control
of the slave-owners and then the succeeding major
party fell under the control of leading business interests. Neither party was ever under control of the
rank-and-file voters.

If the American system is democratic then it is indirectly so and responsive only to very active participants, few of them democrats. The system effectively
shuts most people out of the decision-making process,

which is what the original framers wanted to do. Anybody can see what would happen if the general populace had an effective hand: chaos.

The virtue of the system is that some sort of fairly cohesive policy is always achieved, albeit at more or less heavy cost to justice and equity and also at extra cost to tax-payers.

The reason that justice and equity suffer under the system, at least partially, is that the system caters at all times to special-interest groups. And those special-interest groups that win out do so at the expense of others that are less well financed or less numerous. Most of the populace, in fact, is left out of the dealing with special interests. The populace merely pays more for products or pays more taxes than it otherwise would. The process is one of milking the entire populace for the benefit of the special interests favored by the government.

Here are the mechanics of this process:

Each citizen has one vote for every office. In actuality seldom do more than half of eligible voters vote, and these only on the federal level. When the voting is only for state or municipal offices the voter turnout is much smaller. Voter abstention is usually blamed on apathy, but it is more probably induced by the fact that those who abstain see no personal advantage in either contender.

Most voters habitually vote for one party so that on the federal level the strict party voters are usually about 40 per cent for each party. This leaves 20 per cent of participants independent and it is with this approximate 20 per cent that the decision lies. The side that gets just 11 per cent or slightly more than half the independent vote will usually win.

Here the importance of relatively small pressure-groups is apparent. A sliver group of only 1 or 2 per cent can win a national election.

There is an essentially similar pattern in states for the senatorial vote and in congressional districts.

While there is much talk of ideology during elections, just about all the candidates are merely professional job-hunters, with very little about their outlook partaking of a political philosophy. One hears the word "philosophy" a great deal in elections but rarely encounters the substance itself.

The job of Senator or Congressman is worth about $500,000 per year for each seat, taking in salaries, expense allowances, retirement provisions and a long string of cut-rate services in the style of the special buying privileges of the Soviet *nomenklatura*. On top of all this each candidate is allowed to collect campaign funds running into the millions of dollars and to keep these funds if he does not run again. Presidential candidates get public campaign funds, which match whatever they can collect by passing the hat.

The courts have held that every candidate has a "right" to collect such funds and every citizen has a "right" to give them. What good does it do any giver? It is vociferously denied that contributing funds influences legislation or the enforcement of laws and it is hard to prove that they do. At most, it is said, the donor gains "access" to officeholders.

Any direct donation made to insure governmental action in favor of the donor is considered a bribe and can land the law-maker or official in jail. It was direct bribes to obtain contracts that led to the scandals in Italy.

But the blameless campaign donations in the United States certainly have the effect of making the recipients feel especially friendly to the donors and less likely to pass legislation or to make rulings that are adverse to the interests of the donors. In short, the donations are at least insurance against hostile action toward some interest by officialdom. They are at least that and may also be stimulus to affirmative action on behalf of the donor. Some donors give insurance money to both parties!

Most American citizens rarely encounter donors to political campaigns, which are largely funded by corporate people or organizations. What the donations do is at the very least to guarantee the maintenance of the status quo and may in fact smooth the way to affirmative action of some sort. In some quarters campaign donations are styled as "grease."

Money, in other words, rules the roost all the way. Emerson in the mid-nineteenth century observed that American politics had become a trade, a method of making a living or even a fortune. And so it is. The role of any sort of philosophy in making any kind of political decision is minimal.

Most of the officeholders, especially those who continuously hold one office or the other, belong to a class that in Europe would be considered aristocrats. On this basis the United States has two lines of aristocracy: serial long-term officeholders, and moneyed people. All they lack that their European counterparts have is titles of rank.

As to democracy itself, while it may be discerned here and there in American life, it only partially shows itself in the governmental process.

Legislation that is of special benefit to special interests and is produced by legislative manipulation can hardly be called democratic. However, by agreement among themselves, congressmen call anything they do for a constituent democratic. Support for special interests, however, is not even support for constituencies.

What benefits do special interests get from government action? First, they get direct government subsidies for doing or not doing something. The next valuable benefit is lucrative tax deductions obtained by harmonizing some economic activity with a particular government program. Example: by locating one's production in Puerto Rico a company gains tax advantages.

The rationale for all of this as far as the public is concerned is that it creates jobs, although moving production to Puerto Rico simply moves jobs off the mainland. A defense of each program is some slogan that puts any objector in the position of a dog-in-the-manger or worse. Thus the slogan in defense of the government farm-support program is that it will save the "family farm." Actually since government supports were introduced, family farms have dwindled in number drastically. They've been replaced by corporations (or agribusiness, as it is styled). These now get the support money.

The farm program provides for "support prices" for a wide range of agricultural products. That is to say, if the market price falls below this support level, the government enters the market and buys the product. Then it stores it in one of numerous warehouses.

When, as and if the market price rises, the government sells part or all of what it owns on the open market. If the market price does not rise, the government retains the product indefinitely, at considerable storage cost and eventually absorbs large losses.

As a result of this policy some people take up the production of certain items, adding to market saturation. This has been especially true with peanuts and honey, both of which are in great over-supply. Government warehouses are heavily stocked with honey even while store shelves are stocked with imported honey which is cheaper. Peanuts are similarly in over-supply.

From time to time government food stocks, especially grain, are sold abroad or exported as a form of foreign aid. Much is also released into the American market for the indigent or reputedly indigent in exchange for government-issue food stamps.

Some citizen groups object to the government making foreign loans and grants-in-aid in the belief that money is being sent abroad. But very little money is sent as the funds in payment are used to buy American goods for export.

Whatever politicians can justify as providing jobs for Americans is apt to meet with popular approval for the reason that a large section of American people fear being thrown out of work. The reason for this fear is that without money, one is in serious straits in American society and totally without status. The large number of dependents on government financial assistance represent a sorry assortment of disoriented humanity.

Nor are job prospects for Americans improved by the steady immigration—700,000 arrivals per year legally and about 300,000 per year illegally. Resistance to stopping the flow of illegals comes mainly from the agricultural bloc, which is interested in obtaining cheap field labor for certain crops. The flow of illegals is encouraged by elements associated with the agricultural bloc.

This bloc is very powerful and is centered in the Senate. It controls the votes of all senators who come from agricultural states, which includes just about all of the Middle West. Nothing whatever that this bloc opposes can get through the Senate. Every state has some agricultural activity.

What this constant flow of unskilled immigrants does is to dilute the bargaining power of native

American workers and do some of them out of jobs. Many of the immigrants also swell the welfare rolls and strain the social services.

All through this century, newspaper readers have been regaled with reports of new labor-saving inventions. The reading public rarely realized that labor saving meant job elimination, but such is the case. So, as the population has increased through immigration and births, the number of available jobs has greatly diminished, especially jobs for the unskilled. The number of job-eliminating machines runs into scores and the number of jobholders deprived of employment into millions.

Those who point out such facts fare poorly in American esteem, because the United States functions under a cult of mindless optimism. To incur the ire of this cult is to be marked down as an unpatriotic knocker, not far removed from an atheistic communist. Those who demur are at least stigmatized as unwelcome pessimists although between optimism and pessimism there is another position: realism. And realism is roundly detested in practically all political quarters.

Despite all the political hullabaloo about delivering the moneyless and jobless classes from poverty, the prospects for this seem very, very dim, especially as there is little if any cooperation from the poor. Most of the poor are too unskilled, too uneducated and too feckless to work themselves out of poverty.

It is often popularly stated that in the U.S. system, "the majority rules." Actually the minority often rules. While blocs with a large number of voting members, like the agricultural bloc, often can run their own policies through in the form of laws, very small bodies often can do the same thing.

An obscure group of entities that "knows" some Senator or Congressman can have this single influential individual force a policy on the country. This is done in a simple way, merely by attaching the measure as an amendment to an appropriation bill. Every appropriation bill that passes Congress has enough irrelevant amendments attached to it to make a long tail to a very large kite. Whenever such a bill loaded with special amendments is presented to a President he must sign it in order to get the appropriation for necessary government operations. If he vetoes the bill, a shut-down of a large segment of the government would ensue. As he doesn't want this to happen he signs the bill with all the amendments.

To close this glaring hole in the Constitution there has been proposed a line-item veto for the President, so that he could strike unwanted items off the bill before signing it. Congress has already refused to pass a proposed line-item amendment to the Constitution and it may be predicted that it will continue to do so until there is the point of a bayonet, literally or figuratively, at the throat of every congressman who refuses to sign it.

The line-item veto is one of those obscure technical proposals that does not get much attention but its absence from the Constitution is something that costs taxpayers each year billions of dollars for frivolous and wasteful projects that benefit only a small number of people.

There is nothing "democratic" about this or, indeed, about any phase whatever of the legislative process, which operates by bargain and agreement, a process of log-rolling and back-scratching among the office-retentive legislators.

My entire point is that the United States is not a democracy, as the framers of the Constitution decided. It may be argued that changes have taken place since 1787 and this is true. Senators since 1913 are elected by the populace rather than by state legislatures but they still hold office for six years or long enough to make their tenure permanent. Also, the President is now directly elected by the people rather than by the Electoral College as originally intended. But, once elected, he cannot be removed by the electorate, which has no direct leverage over him.

I say this not in the belief that democratic control would make it better. It would, in my opinion, make it worse. In any event, the system, if at all democratic, is at best indirectly and marginally democratic.

The Italian system, for example, is far more democratic. For in that system an entire government may be voted by parliament out of office, as has happened many times since the end of World War II. The electorate may vote on divisive questions in plebiscites. Thus the electorate, against strong opposition, first voted to permit legal divorce, then legalized the use of birth-control methods and finally legalized abortion on demand. Americans get such boons, if at all, through court interpretations of the Constitution. For Americans to get them by direct legislative action is extremely difficult if not impossible.

Additional Legislative Irregularities

Every congressman is a potential messenger from some special interest to the appointed or permanent officials in every division of the government. Congressmen constantly relay special requests to such officials, often obtaining affirmative action on behalf of the special interest.

The special interests, it is true, may represent a considerable part of the public, directly or indirectly, so the results of their work in Washington may not be as narrowly placed as might at first seem. Nevertheless, all this subterranean activity in Congress, out of sight and unknown to the public, clearly distorts the mission of the government in assuring even-handed justice and equity to the entire populace. Justice and equity are clearly distorted, if not wholly, at least significantly.

There is no way of telling how much distortion. But dominant elements are clearly favored in the process. Perhaps this is a good thing for everybody, but it is hardly in conformity with democratic doctrine.

It is my opinion that the federal court system does the best work toward producing justice and equity, despite a few mistakes from time to time. There have been very few scandals involving federal judges of all levels, in sharp contrast with elected state judges.

The judiciary of the states is riven from time to time by fantastic scandal, especially in the more populous states such as New York, Illinois and California. The state judiciaries are turned toward injustice owing to the need of the incumbents not to offend with their decisions large voting groups in a heterogenous populace.

Most of the original thirteen states, with a few additional, have appointive judges the same as the federal government. And in these states, as on the federal level, there is far less scandal and corruption than in the elective judiciaries.

The presidency itself is ambiguous as far as popular reliability is concerned. One can tell which presidents are less highly thought of than others by the fact that their names are seldom mentioned by commentators and never as models to be followed. The "good" presidents are mentioned most often: Washington, Lincoln, Franklin D. Roosevelt and Harry Truman. The latter is often roundly praised, even by Republicans. "Bad" presidents, like Warren G. Harding, are hardly ever spoken of except in a cautionary way.

Most recent presidents are rated by observers as at least mediocre if not worse. Such are Kennedy, Lyndon Johnson, Nixon, Ford and Carter. I pass over

Reagan and Bush as still subject to partisan evaluation.

Eisenhower is rated as acceptable. The low rating of Herbert Hoover is undeserved as he had little to do with economic events during his term. He took office on March 4, 1929, and the stock market collapsed in late October through no fault of his. What responsibility there was for economic conditions in 1929 and afterwards clearly lay at the doors of Woodrow Wilson, Harding and Calvin Coolidge. It was under Coolidge that the great stock market speculation began.

During his time in office, Coolidge was constantly asked by reporters whether bank loans to stock brokers were too high (which they were) and he repeatedly said they were not too high. It was with these loans that the stock market boom was fueled. Coolidge knew less about the dynamism of events apparently than did the corner shoe shine boy.

During this entire period, all the presidents—Wilson, Harding, Coolidge, Hoover and then Roosevelt—were constantly derided as bumbling nincompoops by New York intellectuals, led by H. L. Mencken. The course of events steadily seemed to justify the derisive scoffing of the intellectuals. Had it not been for World War II, Roosevelt would very probably have been pronounced a failed president rather than one in a Pantheon of four, bracketed with Washington, Lincoln, and Truman. Roosevelt, however, despite his illness was undeniably competent.

What all presidents require in addition to competence is a little bit of luck. Hoover lacked this.

As to Congress, history shows that the presidency always ranges in occupation from rogues to quasi-saints, with the average tending to the low side.

To all of this, cultic patriots may object. Patriotism itself may take various forms. The most approved form of patriotism is the militant type, as celebrated in all national anthems, dedicated to war and only war.

Woodrow Wilson is the one American in history who inflicted the most damage on the United States and, indeed, on western civilization. Ironically, he was also the most educated of the presidents, his area of expertise being political science.

Woodrow Wilson was pro-British from the outset of World War I. He and his administration lied roundly to the American people in order to get them into the war. Every one of the 180,144 American military deaths and 198,150 wounded in that war should be laid at the door of Wilson and Congress. Indeed, if World War II is considered a consequence of World War I, as seems to be the case, Wilson and his administration are initially responsible for its greater damage in lost lives.

Additionally, Wilson discarded without apology the salutary policy of staying clear of entangling alliances that had prevailed since Washington's time. The United States became entangled and remains entangled to this day in a network of alliances that is liable to lead to war at any moment.

Wilson's intention to help Great Britain backfired,

and led instead to the destruction of the British Empire, a loss to the more backward people of the world. By promising to come to the aid of Britain and France he led those countries to reject peace overtures by Germany in 1916.

This rejection led to the Bolshevik revolution as Germany intensified its war against Russia, and ultimately to a punitive peace forced upon already half-starved Germany. This peace, enabled Hitler and the extreme nationalists to re-mobilize Germany for World War II and generated a war in which Britain and France both lost their empires, a course of events which lent color to the Greek concept of Nemesis humbling the arrogant.

The role of Wilson and his aides in guiding the United States into war is the greatest instance of malfeasance in American government. Wilson, of course, meant no harm. As with much wrongdoing, the wrongdoer intends only good.

In extenuation of Wilson's bad judgment was the fact that he suffered from a serious cerebral condition which, however, he carefully hid from the public and from his principal backers. It is a defect of the Constitution that enables candidates for president to conceal ill health, an incident of frequent occurrence in presidents.

As Lord Acton put it, "Power corrupts." Power itself tends to cause the loss of a sense of proportion, to predispose a ruler to think he is something of a deity.

Every official position carries with it a certain area of discretion. How this discretion is used, and how much of it, determines the officeholder's reputation in history.

A Note On Congress

Many weekly American television programs frequently focus on malfeasance in Congress. Such programs are *Prime Time, 20/20, Nightline, 60 Minutes* and a variety of others. The net conclusion to be drawn from these programs, all watched by millions of people, is that there are steady, planned raids on the United States Treasury by outside interests who are aided by blocs of congressmen who in turn are rewarded by legalized bribery (a phrase used in one of the programs).

By way of reaction to such programs, the public opinion of Congress as disclosed in polls, is very low. And although the public as a whole has a low opinion of Congress and of congressmen in general, polls nevertheless show that in each congressional district and state the public holds its representatives and senators in high esteem.

The apparent reason for this one-sided difference in reaction to Congress as a whole and to one's own congressmen and senators is that the officeholders have delivered plenty of so-called "pork" to the home districts and states. Yet it is precisely the voting of so much "pork" or useless but expensive projects, that brings Congress as a whole into such disrepute and places such a burden on taxpayers. What the voters seem to be saying in approving their own congress-people to the exclusion of others is that "pork" is desirable for themselves but reprehensible for others. In brief, the voters themselves are involved in this general conspiracy against the public weal.

An illustration of interlocking conspiracies between legislators and constituents came to light in 1993 with respect to the New York State Assembly. There had been substantial charges that welfare recipients in certain districts were receiving seven or eight welfare checks regularly through fraudulent enrollments. To frustrate these public defrauders it was proposed to install in banks a Japanese-made machine that could instantly verify the validity of any fingerprint. It was also proposed that all welfare recipients be fingerprinted, enabling them to collect one check but preventing the payment of more than one at a time to each recipient.

Upon considering this proposal, the state assembly rejected it on the reported ground that the installation of the fingerprinting system would arouse so much ire among welfare recipients, especially among the defrauders and their friends, that they would vote against incumbent legislators.

In the course of the debate it was pointed out that some of the welfare defrauders collected thousands of dollars per year, all tax free. The proposed measure was dropped.

Hostility towards the common weal, in other

words, is not unique among legislators or government officials. It is also rampant among the public. This fact was well illustrated during World War II by members of the quartermaster's corps in Europe, who were found to be selling military supplies, mainly food, into the black market. The military authorities uncovered several such rings devoted to diverting government property into the profitable black market.

Professional prosecutors and police often come to the apparently cynical conclusion that there is a bit of larceny in everybody. What they are seeing is a return to nature in socialized people. This is the very essence of Hume's idea of natural depravity: a failure to observe the rules of society, which are artificial and often an obstacle to satisfying individual appetites and desires.

It is, however, essential for the preservation of life in society that there be general observance of the rules. It is very probable as far as American society is concerned that much of its dislocation on the lower levels has its origin in failures on the higher levels to obey the laws in the greatest possible detail. When members of the lower orders see members of the upper classes, government officials and the wealthy, disobeying laws, the lower orders take this to signal a general holiday from law observation. Now anything and everything goes.

The Futility of Political Reform

From time to time, reform movements arise and sweep new people into office. Reformers in the United States stepped into power in 1912, 1932 and occasionally later. Kennedy and Johnson both considered themselves reformers.

The efforts of the reformers remind one very strongly of the theme in the novel *Thais* by Anatole France, a mordant fantasy. Thais, an Egyptian queen, is leading a profligate life at the head of her lascivious court, where everything is in a constant whirl. A Christian monk, Paphnutius, in contemplation of this spectacle, decides to convert the queen to Christianity. He is introduced into court circles, meets the queen and enters upon his mission. After a period of time the monk is successful, the queen is converted to Christianity, and becomes a thoroughly chaste person. But in the meantime Paphnutius has been seduced by the wanton attractions of court life and has become a devotee of all the behavior he originally condemned. He tried to de-convert her and attempted to seduce her. Thais and Paphnutius thus exchanged moral roles.

It is this way in government. The reformers usually become addicted to the fleshpots of office and wind up filling the roles of those they originally condemned and displaced. After all the hullabaloo, what did the New Deal accomplish except to increase the public debt, produce a ballooning inflation and a large body of social dependents? Other than its large welfare programs, what is basically different today about the United States from the 1920s? To this question the answer may be more regulation. But the increased regulation does not prevent vast swindles like the building and loan and the urban housing frauds that have cost the taxpayers hundreds of billions of dollars and are costing them billions more in taking over mismanaged banks and defaulted mortgages of the Housing and Urban Development Administration that were guaranteed by the government.

And what stands behind any government guarantee? The taxpayers and only the taxpayers.

Corporate Crime

As we have seen, a few men in government can cause vast harm by involving their countries in futile war. The debris, human and material of the twentieth century, attests to that.

Outside of government, however, some men at the head of giant corporations are poised to do similar damage to large numbers of people and proceed to do so while fully conscious of what they are doing. Here the eagerness to make large sums of money dims the knowledge of what the law requires.

The files of the United States Department of Justice are bulging with the records of crimes and torts committed in the name of corporations by corporate officers. I will cite only two cases to show something of what takes place despite governmental prohibitions.

First, the case of the Johns-Manville Corporation, originally one of the *Fortune* 500 companies. For many years this company supplied asbestos products for the construction industry. Asbestos is a flexible mineral that has the property of resisting fire, and was used especially for roofing material and the insulation of piping in structures of all kinds, including ships.

But something this company neglected to tell the public, although its records show that it knew it, was that asbestos, if inhaled in the form of dust particles, is extremely dangerous. It induces a fatal disease known as asbestosis. Researchers knew the dangers of this mineral as far back as the 1890s, and company records show that company officers knew of them in the 1930s.

The company could have greatly reduced its liability if it had warned users of the potential dangers of its products. But it did not warn anybody, presumably so as not to inhibit usage and sales.

Sales of the product boomed year after year and increased markedly during World War II when it was used in the insulation of ships being built for military purposes. In the wartime shipyards thousands of workers were exposed to asbestos dust and were never warned to take precautions.

After the war, thousands of former shipyard workers suffered fatal asbestosis. So many suits were filed against the company that it was driven into bankruptcy and ceased to function except as a paying agent to successful claimants.

But the resources of the company were not sufficient to meet all the claims, many of which as of this writing remain unsatisfied. And in the meantime many of the claimants have died.

A large public, alarmed at the asbestos reports, clamored to have it removed from public buildings. A large variety of public buildings, including schools, had ceilings and interior walls of asbestos. But these were now seen as threatening the life and health of people in those buildings, including children.

There ensued, therefore, a vast and expensive program of ripping out asbestos interiors. Television viewers were treated to scenes of masked white-clad workers removing the dreaded material. Steam pipes under the streets of New York City, encased in asbestos, burst at times, spewing asbestos dust and causing great alarm and much removal expense.

All in all, the introduction of this known dangerous substance into society proved to be a prolonged and very costly disaster.

Another case is that of the Continental Can Company, which was accused of operating a huge pension fraud against its workers. In a federal court action the company was charged with systematically laying off elderly workers as they approached the date of their retirement, upon which they were entitled to draw pensions.

Workers at first were not alarmed because the company had a policy of laying off people from time to time, but always re-employing them after a period. But the pattern that was revealed in the class-action lawsuit against the company was that employees approaching retirement age were being permanently laid off, and thus were no longer entitled to retirement pensions.

An event like this, in which a company is ordered to pay $415 million to retirees, makes an interesting and passing news item, but the mere facts conceal all the anguish and hardship suffered for years by hundreds of cheated pensioners, some of whom died before receiving any pension.

Companies use pension plans to retain trusted and steady workers, insuring the regular production of their product. To deal legitimate pensioners out in this underhanded way is to epitomize depravity.

Many other cases similar to that of Johns-Manville and Continental Can could be cited, although some corporations fully meet their obligations to employees and customers. Those who do not, and who break the law, illustrate perfectly Hume's distinction between emphasizing projects of benefit to oneself at the expense of violating the laws.

A particularly callous case of corporation lawlessness came to light in 1993 (See *The New York Times*, October 16, 1993). One of the world's largest medical device manufacturers, C. R. Bard Inc., pleaded guilty to more than 390 counts of fraud and illegal human experimentation for selling unlicensed heart catheters.

The illegal sales resulted in at least one death and caused 22 emergency heart operations. The company was fined $61 million by the government, an amount equal to the gross sales of the defective products. At the same time the chairman of the company and five former officers were charged in a 393-count indictment. The maximum penalty upon conviction is 5 to 20 years in prison and a $250,000 fine on each count. But courts rarely if ever deal harshly with corporate officers and even at times express sympathy for their plight.

There are in fact on the official record thousands of cases of corporate malfeasance. The safest and most lucrative criminal activities take place behind the screen of a corporation.

In cases where a government or corporation violates the law or uses unsound judgment, it affects thousands and in some cases millions of people, making life more difficult for everybody.

Corporate wrongdoing has played a large role in American history. In the latter part of the nineteenth century from the time of the Civil War to about the year 1900, there were practically no federal restrictions on corporations, which did what they pleased. But soon after 1900 there was a change in the national mood, attributable in some degree to critical writings. An especially influential book was Upton Sinclair's *The Jungle* (1904), which described conditions in the Chicago stockyards and slaughterhouses. There were many other books and magazine articles of the same sensationally revelatory nature. In response to the flood of writings President Theodore Roosevelt called their authors "muckrakers," illogically blaming the diagnosticians for the disease.

The realistic scenes of life in the Chicago stockyards described by Sinclair were largely instrumental for the passage of the United States Food and Drug Act in 1906. In ensuing years there were many other reforms.

The Food and Drug Act has been many times amended to make it more rigorous. As to drugs, prior to this act, many entrepreneurs throughout the country would mix dubious potions, bottle them and peddle them as cure-alls by the wagonload. The products were eagerly purchased by a gullible population. But the potions had no curative properties whatever.

This form of marketing was ended by new federal legislation to combat over-the-counter sales of a variety of patent medicines that were found to be inert or directly harmful.

The United States today has strict drug laws, for which the public can thank the muckrakers. It also maintains federal supervision over the production of foodstuffs, although recent investigations have shown that food inspection is badly flawed. For one thing, federal laws do not apply to intrastate production and distribution of food products. Also inspection of slaughterhouses has been found to be lax.

Television has shown carcasses falling off overhead transport mechanisms and being picked up off dirty floors and replaced on the machinery that transports them to the system delivering them to customers. Inspection has revealed such carcasses to be infected and dangerous to consumers. From time to time, incidents of meat-poisoning through restaurant food have become public.

Apart from food and drugs, other corporate operations have come to be restricted, as by the Securities and Exchange Commission established under the New Deal. Thanks to the application of the Securities and Exchange Act, there have been many corporate and stock-market scandals as some business people failed to realize the country now has laws with teeth in them. Fines running into hundreds of millions of dollars in individual cases have been levied by the government.

Corporations and business people have been convicted for a long litany of crimes: tax evasion, bribery, false labelling, deceptive practices, patent infringement, monopoly, false advertising, adulteration of product, unfair labor practices, dumping of noxious substances, improper safety practices, unfair competition, and so on.

Nor are loose business practices confined to the United States. Italy is steeped in business-political corruption and all the other crimes one finds in the United States. Orderly Japan, too, has experienced a series of corporate-political scandals. There is corporate infringement of the law in all countries where corporations operate.

Official Failure to Protect

Although it is the settled role of government to protect its citizens, many public officials in a variety of ways have been as delinquent as corporate officials in protecting the public from gross harm. In the matter of the development of nuclear energy in particular, it is notable that public officials have defaulted on their trust.

Ever since the inception of nuclear energy, officials in many countries, and especially in the United States, failed to insure that workers and people living near nuclear process plants were protected. There was failure, too, in everybody from presidents on down in protecting the American people from nuclear fall-out.

At the first step, the men who mined uranium were not informed that their work was especially dangerous. The result was that many of these men later suffered from the effects of radiation.

Next, in processing plants spread around the country, workers were not fully informed of the dangers. Many safety measures were neglected or omitted. It was the same, too, in various plants making nuclear weapons.

All in all, an unknown number of people were exposed to radiation, with what total effect is not known. At the same time the populace adjacent to nuclear plants had no knowledge that anything dangerous was going on in their vicinity.

The rationale for the general silence was "patriotism." It was reasoned that dispatch was necessary in all phases of the nuclear program in a strategy that would fail if warnings were posted and enforced. The program, it was felt, was necessary in order to defend against a menacing Soviet Union.

Meanwhile in the Soviet Union the handling of nuclear materials was even more careless, with catastrophic consequences for large segments of the population.

In essence government officials, from different motives, resembled Johns-Mansville Corporation officials, in failing to warn workers and neighbors of the dangers involved and the need for special precautions.

The people in charge of nuclear programs felt that if anyone was injured through ignorance of what was going on it was a price to be paid—by others—for the sake of patriotism.

Political Corruption: World-Wide and in the U.S.A.

Political corruption is found in all cultures, among all systems of government and under all ideologies. It is, in short, a universal characteristic of men and governments, one that validates Hume's precept about the difficulty of obeying man-made laws even though they are necessary to human survival.

Basically, political corruption consists of the unlawful misuse of public office for personal gain, the illegal purchase of votes, promises of office or special favors in return for money, coercion, falsification, intimidation, and interference with free elections. The object of all participants is personal gain at the expense of the commonalty.

The United States has never experienced pervasive corruption from top to bottom, as was recently reported from Italy. Rather it has been sporadic and episodic, sometimes on the federal level, at other times on the state or, most often, municipal levels.

On the federal front historians have focused on the Yazoo land frauds of 1795, the case of the second Bank of the United States, the operations of the nineteenth-century political machines of William Marcy Tweed, Thurlow Weed and Simon Cameron and the crookedness of Reconstruction legislatures and their ostensibly redeeming successors. The entire administration of President Grant turned out to be corrupt to an extent not equalled until the Harding Administration of the early 1920s which saw at least one cabinet officer imprisoned. Both these episodes showed there was no limit to how far some corrupters would go in attaining their ends. In every war, too, there has been extensive corruption in the procurement of military supplies.

Certain cases of corruption stand out in their magnitude. One of these was the Credit Mobilier scandal of 1872. Credit Mobilier of America was the construction company for the Union Pacific Railroad, to which the government provided grants, subsidies and donations of land. As it turned out, many congress-men and other politicians held gifts of stock in Credit Mobilier, to which Union Pacific presented bills for inflated costs to the extent of $50 million, a huge sum in those days.

This overcharge for the benefit of political insiders reminds one of the consistently heavy overcharges by military contractors of all kinds paid out by the Pentagon on behalf of the Defense Department during the Cold War with the Soviet Union. After every war in which the United States has been involved, came revelations of overcharging by contractors in cahoots with friends in the government.

A definitive history of political corruption in the United States would have to include distillations of muckraking books like the following:

Two Years Before the Mast by Richard Henry Dana (1840)

Chapters of Erie by Charles Francis Adams (1871)

History of the Standard Oil Company by Ida Tarbell (1902). (This book provided most of the data that led to the conviction and dissolution of the company in 1911.)

The Shame of the Cities by Lincoln Steffens (1904)

The Jungle by Upton Sinclair (1904)

Frenzied Finance by Thomas William Lawton (1905)

The Treason of the Senate by David Graham Phillips (1906)

The following five books by Gustavus Myers:

The History of the Great American Fortunes, 3 vols. (1910); *The History of Public Franchises in New York* (1900); *History of the United States Supreme Court* (1912); *History of Tammany Hall* (1901); *History of Bigotry in the United States* (1943).

The Robber Barons by Matthew Josephson (1934)

The Muckraker Years (1974) and *The Social and Political Ideas of the Muckrakers* (1964) by David M. Chalmers

The Muckrakers and American Society by Herbert Shapiro (1968)

The Muckrakers: Crusading Journalists by Fred Cook (1972)

Muckraking: Past, Present and Future by John M. Harrison (1973)

Muckraker by John Parsons Peditto (1976)

The Muckrakers: The Era in Journalism That Moved America to Reform (The most significant magazine articles 1902 to 1912) by Arthur Weinberg (1961)

Muckraking Sociology: Research As Social Criticism by Gary T. Marx (1972)

Theodore Roosevelt denounced the first group of these writers as "muckrakers." The president, himself a political mountebank and show-off, took this term from John Bunyan's *The Pilgrim's Progress*, wherein the Man with the Muck-Rake is so preoccupied with raking filth from the ground that he cannot see the celestial crown being offered him. Roosevelt, presumably, like many politicians, thought he was already in possession of that crown.

The writings of the muckrakers came as a surprise to most newspaper readers because the press did not ordinarily feature this sort of material until well after the muckrakers' writings appeared in print. And although the muckraking movement subsided with the advent of World War I, it revived with the Depression of 1930-40 and continues strongly today as a general exposé and revelation movement. The muckrakers unloaded on the nation a deluge of largely scandalous revelations about leading personages and institutions. Many of these revelations led to long overdue concrete reforms.

There is a running propaganda of self-praise in the United States originating with the first Fourth of July celebration. Immigrants are regularly interviewed on television about the beauties of freedom in the United States as compared with the restrictions where they came from. The interviewers, however, never bring out that in the United States there is a free-lance semi-guerrilla class of criminals which yearly affects adversely some one-third of American families.

In many foreign countries a person can be arrested and perhaps tortured or killed simply for disapproving of the regime. This cannot happen in the United States. But in the United States a person can be robbed, injured or killed, for no reason at all. Under the extremely liberal American legal system many career criminals, with the aid of defense lawyers, lead apparently charmed lives of crime.

United States Senator Phil Gramm, Republican of Texas, in *The New York Times* on July 8, 1993 cited data gathered by a Texas economist to the effect that in 1990 the chances of criminals being convicted and imprisoned were remote.

These data showed that "on average, a person committing murder in the United States can expect to spend only 1.8 years in prison. For rape, the expected punishment is 60 days. Expected time in prison for robbery is 23 days, 6.7 days for arson and 6.4 days for aggravated assault. And for stealing a car, a person can reasonably expect to spend just a day and a half in prison."

It is not just the liberality of judges that brings such light treatment of dangerous criminals. For one thing, the prisons are full and the taxpayers in many states object to spending more money on housing criminals. But the taxpayers will either have to do this or endure the depredations of vicious elements.

In short, life in the United States is not as rosy as many immigrants seem to believe. For a large section of the populace, and this is especially true for newcomers, life can be very difficult.

The rising tide of crime will not be stopped until public protests really frighten politicians. Right now the national homicide rate is about 25,000 annually, which is approximately five times the American death-rate in ten years of the Vietnam War. But the prevalent reluctance to impose the death penalty for murder does much to negate the authority of the government and to encourage wrongdoers who conclude that the government is unaccountably afraid to punish them.

Eventually government in the United States will be obliged to deal far more forcefully than it does with the problem of violent crime as well as of insidious non-violent crime.

People who believe the age of the muckrakers is at an end aren't aware of the large body of exposé literature that has developed since 1930 nor are they aware that the paragon of muckraking books, published in 1993, is titled *Official and Confidential: The Secret Life of J. Edgar Hoover* by Anthony Summers, an English writer. This book establishes that the master criminal of all time in the United States was J. Edgar Hoover, founder and director of the Federal Bureau of Investigation. The FBI was actually founded in 1908 but remained an insignificant agency until 1924 when Hoover was appointed director. He immediately began expanding it until it reached nearly 20,000 employees.

As director of the F.B.I., Hoover was the chief law-enforcement officer of the United States. The agency was in charge of enforcing all federal laws except those especially assigned to agencies like the post office, the Bureau of Alcohol, Tobacco and Firearms and the Customs Office. Throughout his long tenure, Hoover could decide whom to proceed against and whom to ignore.

He was reappointed by every president until his death in 1972. Presidents were afraid not to reappoint him because of all the information he had. Hoover brought information to every president, thereby impressing him with his information-gathering ability. In 1939 President Roosevelt had, by executive order, given Hoover authority to track down political subversives in the United States. With this authority Hoover tapped government telephones in Washington, including those of members of Congress.

Whenever he obtained damaging information about any public official, Hoover would notify that official via messenger and assure him that the information would be kept confidential. In this way Hoover obtained implicit power over just about everybody in government. He used this power to fortify his position as head of the F.B.I., making himself impregnable and irremovable.

But, as Summers brings out, Hoover had a weakness that made him potentially vulnerable. He was a closet homosexual and transvestite who became so careless in attending orgies that he found himself photographed in homosexual situations. Some of these photographs found their way to leaders of the Mafia, including Meyer Lansky, and gave the Mafia a tacit hold over him. As a result of this hold, Hoover took the position, often publicly stated, that there was no national Mafia in the Unites States, contrary to all evidence. His stated belief was that any Mafia activity was purely local and outside federal jurisdiction.

Under this theory, the national Mafia flourished. While many observers disputed Hoover's views about the localism of Mafia activities, in 1957 there was disclosed a big meeting of Mafia chieftans from all over the country at Appalachin, N.Y. In response, Hoover allowed the F.B.I. to report that there was indeed a national Mafia but the report was suppressed.

Hoover, in fact, was the master-protector of the Mafia owing to their power of blackmail over him, the very kind of power that kept him in office under succeeding presidents.

The author of this book interviewed more than 800 people to gather his materials, took full advantage of published documentation and used the Freedom of Information Act to get at F.B.I. files. The index of names in the book becomes something like a criminal directory of high circles in Washington, D.C., during the years of Hoover's reign. Anyone who has not read this book cannot know what went on in Washington during the years 1924 to 1972.

Hoover was a close friend and orgy-mate of Lewis S. Rosenstiel, head of Schenley Distillers and a former illegal importer of alcohol under Prohibition. He was referred to by Meyer Lansky and other upper Mafia figures as "Supreme Commander," and was a key figure in the control of organized crime. It was mainly through Rosenstiel that Hoover had his connection with organized crime, also known as the Mafia and The Syndicate.

According to Summers Hoover was a tremendous "free-loader." He signed chits all around, at hotels, restaurants and resorts, but was never presented with a bill. He also constantly received expensive gifts from very wealthy and influential people. The way the Mafia paid Hoover for omitting it from the governmment agenda was as follows: Hoover and his fellow-homosexual assistant, Clyde Tolson, were close followers of horse races. Hoover, through intermediaries, would place big bets. If he lost he was never called upon to pay, but if he won the bets were paid.

Hoover's entire operation apparently took place without explicit agreements. As far as the record shows he never blackmailed anyone or threatened to do so, but people knew he had politically destructive information about them. He probably never asked for his free-loading or betting arrangements, which simply developed "naturally." Probably nobody could ever truthfully testify that Hoover had ever agreed to do anything wrong. He just did it. Merely neglecting to go after the Mafia, if it was done with malice or thought of profit, was a serious federal offense.

The Power of Muckraking

Muckraking in American life is an outgrowth of the original puritanical character of its society. In the course of time, most publishers deferred to this attitude by adopting a genteel approach to public expression. As the newspaper developed, some of this attitude was put aside, but not entirely. Publishers took the stand that theirs were "family newspapers" and therefore could not deal with certain delicate matters. The motto of *The New York Times* is a holdover from those days: "All the news that's fit to print," satirized as "all the news that fits *we* print."

The paternalism of the press made it amenable to manipulation. Reporters used to be reproved for trying to publish matter unfit for a "family newspaper." Such material was edited out. Chief Justice John Marshall of the United States Supreme Court once said, "The power to tax is the power to destroy." In paraphrase of that statement one can say "The power to edit is the power to distort."

By editing out material puritanically deemed unfit—mainly sexual in nature—the American press found itself in a position where it could also edit out material displeasing to advertisers, bankers and industrialists. The press became a general propaganda medium in defense of the status quo, as shown during the New Deal years. It was into this situation that the muckrakers stepped. Their books derived power from the information vacuum in which they appeared.

The muckrakers were not interested in sexual peccadillos, and none of their books dealt with them. What they dealt with was gross public wrongdoing and abuse of authority for profit.

In the case of J. Edgar Hoover, what he knew about the private lives of public officials was probably of little public importance although it was of vital importance to an elected official in coping with a puritanic electorate. However, sexual accusations have lost most of their power, as was shown in the 1992 presidential campaign for Bill Clinton, who won despite a rash of sexual accusations.

The general vacuum in the news reports and the puritanical background is what gives the Summers book on Hoover its explosive force. For the material in the book was available all along, as the author shows, although most of it was never published in newspapers where Hoover's inherent criminality was never hinted at. Hoover, instead, was presented by the press as an icon of law and order, a crime-fighter par excellence.

At his death Hoover's body was put on view in State in the national Capitol building, the first time anyone except a dead president has been so honored. Perhaps it was done in unconscious recognition of the fact that Hoover presided over presidents. And after his death the new building of the Department of Justice was named the J. Edgar Hoover building, perhaps in recognition of the fact that even in death his name was still awesome to a corrupted officialdom.

All of the muckraking and exposé literature is documentation for Hume's thesis that mankind in general has difficulty following the rules laid down by civilized societies. But everyday observation of people in public life shows that many of them seem oblivious to even the mildest rules.

Looking Backward

In characterizing the twentieth century as the most destructive in history it is not suggested that mankind in the last century suddenly became worse than usual. On the contrary, man was just being himself through the entire century. There was, however, a change in his circumstances. In the first place he possessed new weapons of vast destructive power: dynamite, TNT, gasoline, airplanes, armored vehicles, submarines, torpedoes, the atom and hydrogen bombs. All this was backed up by powerful industrial establishments. With all these instrumentalities put into use man had the means to achieve wholesale destruction, and he used those means lavishly.

Furthermore, there was now an abundance of people on earth, which meant there were many more present to be slaughtered and tortured. The population of the earth had grown enormously since the beginning of the eighteenth century, thanks to improvements in science, agriculture, medicine and sanitation.

In the year 1 A.D. demographers estimate that world population was 200 to 300 millions of people, thinly scattered. Back in this period was developed the concept of the sacredness of human life, expressed in religious contexts and asserted in the laws of civilized nations. But the sense of the sacredness of human life dissipated with the rapid increase of population.

By the year 1600, according to the United Nations, world population had approximately doubled to around 500 million. Of this population about 20 per cent was in Europe and 60 per cent in Asia with the other 20 per cent in Africa and Latin America.

From a total of 508 million world-wide in 1650, of which 106 million were in Europe and the USSR regions, the world total rose to 3,592 million (or 3.6 billion) in 1970. Of that total 700 million were in Europe and USSR, 227 million in the United States and Canada and 2,646 million in so-called developing countries, mainly in Asia. "Developing countries" is a phrase used to replace "backward countries."

United Nations projections foresee a world population of 6,130 million (6.1 billion) people by the year 2000 A.D., of which 354 million will be in North America, 880 million in Europe and USSR regions and 3,458 million (3.4 billion) in Asia. China, India, Indonesia and the rest of Asia are expected to increase the most.

The population of China alone at this writing is 1.2 billion and the Chinese government, in rational defense, has decreed that no woman may bear more than one child. In protest against this necessary law, many Chinese fleed the country, claiming their human rights had been violated. Offspring in China are traditionally important, as it is by offspring that one is assured spirits of ancestors will be kept alive.

It is against this huge population increase that governments can afford to send men by the hundreds of thousands against machine guns in the name of patriotism. Czarist generals sent thousands of Russian peasants against well-armed Germans. The Russians were armed only with bayonets on bulletless rifles.

The German Nazis devised gas chambers to dispose of thousands of people they deemed unfit to live. The Nazis made no mechanical provision for the disposal of bodies, which had to be carried away by hand, a process economists call labor-intensive. No doubt, given time, the Nazis would have devised a serial method for converting the dead bodies either into electric power or into fertilizer.

All such developments are still to be seen but are by no means impossible, given special regimes and exigencies.

But it has manifestly been the availability of people in large numbers that made it possible, in the name of patriotism, to send millions to early deaths at places like Verdun and Stalingrad, to say nothing of all those blown away in lesser engagements. The availability of surplus manpower obviously is what makes it possible for generals to think in terms of giant battles such as the Battle of the Atlantic, the Battle of Europe and the Battle of the Pacific. There could well be a Battle of Asia or a Battle of Africa, in which gigantic forces converge on each other.

Already atomic bombs and poison-gas bombs are in possession of the United States, Russia, Ukraine, Great Britain, France, China, India and Pakistan. Once the balloon goes up, so to speak, there will be enough fire-power on tap to reduce the world population significantly and possibly leave all survivors poisoned by radiation.

Meanwhile, in the United States, Catholic and other religious factions protest birth-control and abortion, which are the only rational methods of population control other than total sexual abstinence. The fixation of religious elements of all stripes strongly suggests that human procreativeness is closely related to religious ardor.

The steadily increasing population has been paralleled for more than a century by an endless stream of new inventions, all hailed in the press as labor-saving devices. What is overlooked in the celebration of these developments is that the labor-saving is largely at the expense of human occupations, of jobs. So there is imminent prospect of the danger of creating a permanent army of unemployed, who will have to be supported by the employed or allowed to starve. There are already many signs that there has been created an impoverished leisure class.

As of the mid-seventeenth century the average life-expectancy of all new-borns was 25 years. Forty per cent of all new-borns failed to live beyond the first year. With the elimination of sweeping epidemics and the application of scientific medicine all this has changed.

Contrary currents are assailing the human animal worldwide. Favorable developments also bring with them unfavorable outcomes. The increase in the human survival-rate brings with it the threat of over-population and starvation. The increase in technical proficiency produces the threat of joblessness for millions.

In former days huge population buildups, as in Asia today, were forerunners of mass invasions of other lands. Such invasions today are less workable in the light of modern weaponry in the possession of advanced countries although there are noticeable attempts to smuggle people from Asia to North America and Europe. There is, however, an ongoing peaceful invasion of countries like the United States by desperate surplus populations from the Third World.

The obvious remedy is to limit population through birth control and abortion but, as already noted, these are rejected by religious elements.

The Third World Overflows

A visible effect of the migration, legal and illegal, is the emergence in American cities of distinctly Third World sections, sometimes enveloping entire cities such as Newark. The way to Third World status of these cities was preceded by the internal migration of uneducated rural blacks from the agrarian South with the introduction of the mechanical cotton-picker in the 1940s and 1950s.

Into these already black neighborhoods there now poured migrants from abroad, most of them illegal, thus transforming entire areas into fair replicas of Calcutta, Bombay and Shanghai. While all this was happening, politicians stood mainly idly by, some muttering that the United States is a nation of immigrants as though that justified crowding the country beyond its capacity to support the newcomers in a civilized way.

Cities of the United States that have taken on important Third World aspects—over-crowding, street crime, sidewalk peddling, people sleeping in public and on the floors of railroad and bus stations and general littering and spread of debris—are New York, Philadelphia, Boston, Baltimore, a large segment of northeast Washington, D.C., Detroit, Chicago, Milwaukee, St. Louis, Los Angeles, San Francisco, and others.

The state of California seems on the brink of becoming a Third World state because it is the constant recipient of an influx of illegal aliens coming from Latin America through Mexico. As an effect of this invasion public signs in California and in New York City now appear in Spanish as well as English. Such a development never occurred during the European immigrations of the nineteenth and early twentieth centuries. Public signs were not put up in German, Italian, Polish or Yiddish.

The public is rather apathetic toward all this. Except in California, there is a curious relation of the unemployment of nine million people in 1993 with the fact that since the 1960s there has been an immigration of nine million people, many of them illegals. The current legal quota of immigrants is 700,000 annually, of which about one quarter are reported to be college graduates.

All these new immigrants are causing a great strain on the tax structure, especially in California, for the federal government requires that the states educate the children of illegal immigrants and furnish medical care to all immigrants. In California the state treasurer complains that it is costing the state $500 million annually to maintain in prison recent immigrants convicted of crimes. He proposes to establish treaties with the countries of origin, under which such people serve their sentences where they originated, a proposal that will hardly hold water. For anyone returned as a criminal is not likely to be maintained in prison owing to the cost.

What is mainly inducing some Americans to look askance at this whole process is the cost. Europe has similarly been forced to look at the cost of absorbing large numbers of immigrants, many of whom were brought into Germany on an emergency contract basis as defense workers. But when the newcomers, through sheer force of numbers, start changing the entire social and cultural atmosphere, giving it a Third World aspect, there was rising objection. Essentially, Third Worldism consists of living on the streets, in full public view.

Basically, as far as solutions are concerned, there will have to be much more direct control of population, along the lines adopted by the Chinese government. In this policy China is ahead of the whole world.

In extenuation for all the illegal aliens pouring over United States borders and in downplaying the damage they do to American society, it is often said, "we are a nation of immigrants." Even if this were true, it does not follow that the country should be open to entry by all comers as a haven for the entire world.

In the words of many apologists for the illegals it is made to seem they are modern replicas of the Pilgrim Fathers who came to the country. These statements appeal only to a vapid floating sentimentalism. There is, however, little sentimentalism behind the illegal process, which is actually encouraged from inside the United States by our old friends: citizen law-breakers. These are people interested in cheap unskilled labor and in keeping the price of labor low for the benefit of employers. This is where the impetus for illegal immigration comes from.

FAIR (Federation for American Immigration Reform) was established in the 1980s to make the country aware of the problem of illegal immigration, which until then had received little public notice. In its efforts to have remedial measures enacted, FAIR has been opposed by an invisible hand in every legislative body before which it has appeared. The conclusion to be drawn is that those who oppose it are financed by people who are interested in obtaining cheap labor and higher profits—the usual story.

Many employers, indeed, prefer illegals to legal immigrants because the illegals, who are technically outlaws, are in no position to complain about low pay, bad working conditions or lack of benefits. Most illegals in the United States work in unbelievably squalid and degrading conditions. As they are illegal this may be considered a fair tradeoff, but the harm they do in competing with legal workers is incalculable.

In addition to a deluge of illegal immigrants in the United States and certain European countries such as Germany, the United States and no doubt the world is swamped by a deluge of children born out of wedlock.

Under new so-called liberal dispensations the mother of an illegitimate child need not fear lack of support because the government with its welfare laws sees to it that she is not left in the lurch financially. Indeed, it is widely suspected, and probably rightly so, that many young women get pregnant deliberately so that they will be eligible for the welfare rolls and will thereby get a long-term meal-ticket. Some women have a number of illegitimate children (if I may be permitted to use the term) by different and casually known men because with each additional child her monthly welfare check is increased.

In other words, the law as written, unquestionably stimulates the illegitimate birth-rate by enabling the women, many of them teen-agers, to become long-term public charges.

As of mid-1993 the statistics given out by government agencies are as follows: no less than 63 per cent of the births of the black or African-American community are illegitimate while 20 per cent of all white births are illegitimate. This is a recent development.

What this guarantees is that this large number of children will be brought up without fathers and many of them will be reared by local social service systems.

In some cases women alone, with one or more illegitimate children, rear them and some do so with astonishing success. But in many cases the mothers, owing to drug addiction, alcoholism or some other infirmity, must yield the children to social service agencies. These agencies farm out the children, as it were, to low-paid, unskilled foster parents, people themselves in need of income, and some children arrive in their teens after having been in as many as ten foster homes, always with bad results.

And such children are almost always emotionally disturbed, with problems in and out of school—if they attend school at all. They join the large number of abused children from legitimate homes, most of whom soon show themselves as eligible for the underclass of illegal immigrants, alcoholics, drug users and social misfits.

Some with phenomenal luck come through virtually unscathed and establish themselves in some line of legitimate activity. But most do not because they are not properly prepared or acculturated. At age 21 they join the ranks of homeless, until recently called derelicts.

I am not arguing that a woman alone cannot raise a child or two in a satisfactory way. Some strong and inspiring women can do this. But they are exceptions.

Here and there professional women of ample means will have a child out of wedlock, and show that such a child can be properly reared. But that it can be done by an educated woman with ample means is no support for the view that an impoverished girl who knows nothing about child-rearing can do it.

That the public tolerates so much illegality, in producing children and in immigration, hardly stems from permissiveness. Rather it is a sign of indolence, for which the public will pay.

Concluding Evaluations

A survey such as this will have little appeal for those people who, like the three little monkeys, speak no evil, hear no evil and see no evil. Such people, for example, say they do not follow the news reports because they report only bad news, never good.

Actually, news organizations mainly report deviations from existing norms, good or bad with some exclusion of the bad. The reason for the existence of so much bad news is that most of the known deviations are bad, contrary to the laws or to approved circumstances and standard expectancies.

David Hume in the eighteenth century was of the opinion that there was nothing much government could do to keep people approximately obedient to law except to prosecute offenders and punish them, a gloomy view but true for the times. However there have since been technical changes in the world that require some modification of this gloomy view and give us some reason for a mildly optimistic view of the possibilities for improvement.

Often when authors in their writings disclose some undesirable condition, readers ask them to supply a remedy and if they cannot, the writers are dismissed as triflers or sensationalists. But in medicine some doctors discover and outline a disease without being able to state a cure for it and their findings are not therefore dismissed.

In the present case I believe I am able to state a way in which the situation Hume disclosed can at least be modified and ameliorated. As we have seen, Hume noticed that people have difficulty in observing the laws, legal and natural, that are necessary to their survival as a group. He attributed this difficulty not to some inherent wickedness in the characters of people but to a difference in the vividness of their perception as between what immediately affected their personal interests and what the government required of them. What the government required was always far less vivid than any project or enterprise in which a person was engaged.

People, Hume said, had a very vivid apprehension of whatever involved their personal interest but had only a dim vague apprehension of what related to their collective interest—indeed, to their very survival as a group. The laws in general, devised and supervised by the government, were what kept people as a group in line and it was individuals, pursuing their own interest, who broke these laws or failed to observe them. It is by failing to observe the laws or the rules that people default on their social responsibilities.

To modify this difficulty and to bring some improvement into the world I propose that the government make use of modern means of communication like television and radio to impress daily upon people the necessity of living up to the laws. The government could do this by requiring television and radio stations to project "sound bites" among their programs. These would remind people to obey laws in general and also particular laws from time to time. Such "sound bites" would serve as a reminder to all those who wish to support the government in its efforts.

If people responded favorably to such use of television and radio, and if newspapers followed their example, there might be some improvement in affairs.

Naturally, one could not expect murderers, armed robbers, rapists, confidence men, pickpockets and corrupt politicians to respond to such messages but in the matter of local offenses and misdemeanors there might be a vast improvement. Already the media have taken a small step in this direction by issuing warnings against drunk driving. Such warnings should regularly, daily, be issued with respect to laws in general and certain laws in particular.

Sufficient use is not made of radio and television for serious purposes. Both media are largely given over to the presentation of entertainment and product advertising. But that they are not influential cannot be claimed in view of the billions of dollars spent on them in advertising each year. The media are influential in inducing people to buy goods, often very expensive goods, so they should be influential in the suggested respect as well.

But, it might be objected, it would be monotonous to have reminders published every day as "sound bites" to obey laws in general and specifically named laws in particular. This objection cannot be taken seriously in view of all the monotonous material now being published on the electronic media and in newspapers: weather reports, sport reports, news of local crimes, stock market tables and the like. Except for changes of minor details it is the same story day after day. Spectacular and individual news events come only seldom to break the monotony.

And as to reminders to heed the laws the writers

could use their own ingenuity to bring variety and humor into the messages.

Another way to improve law observance is to give special courses in the high schools, which did not exist as far-flung systems in Hume's day.

People in general think of the law simply as a system of restrictions on their personal liberties but fail to see that the laws protect them from many dangers. In the matter of food and drugs, for example, various laws guarantee their purity and specific properties. And in the matter of special skills, such as medicine, the laws guarantee that one will not be tended by a charlatan as was often the case in an earlier day. A special high-school course on law could bring home to students the many protections given them by the laws as they are observed.

As a consequence of such a course in all the high-schools, the social situation, especially in the United States, could be much improved.

As to content such a course, going far beyond civics, could cover a very great deal of interesting material, especially with the citation of cases. Attention would, from time to time, be focused on the difficulty Hume revealed in people, as reported in the law. It would be a course that could not fail to arouse the attention and interest of the dullest student. It could convert many students into strong supporters of the laws.

Now, to reject these suggestions out of hand, without putting them to a test, would seem to me to be a big mistake. It would amount to resigning oneself to the semi-lawless condition that confronts us.

Judging by the fierce way the government goes after offenders against the law, the government wants the laws to be observed, not ignored or scoffed at. Here, then, is a way to obtain greater compliance.

I am not calling for people to inform on others as law-breakers. What I am suggesting is that each patriotic person take heed of the notices that would intermittently appear on radio and television and in newspapers and guide themselves by them.

If people heeded the daily reminders many situations would surely be improved. There might be less littering, less defacing of walls, less reckless and drunken driving, fewer red lights ignored by motorists, less unnecessary noise and fewer assaults in slight cause. There would probably not be much reduction in the major crimes, to which too much personal interest is attached. But even if only minor offenses were reduced there would be much social gain.

Patriotism and Law Observance

People like to be considered patriotic. To show their patriotism they like to march in parades, wave flags, cheer the marchers and in general testify to their fealty to the government. But all such gestures prove little or nothing. One could be a foreign saboteur or terrorist and go through such patriotic motions as part of one's masquerade.

But despite the hosannahs of the politicians to those who have made the supreme sacrifice and to those who have served in uniform, there is no proof of patriotism by others, by civilians much less by the orating politicians.

If one is a patriotic supporter of the government one is, at a minimum, law-abiding at all times. To claim to love the government and the country and not to heed its laws is a contradiction in terms. Illegals who enter the country surreptitiously professing to love it are starting by breaking one of its laws, which hardly argues for supporting it. The illegals who come into this country simply cannot love the government but wish to insinuate themselves into American society in order to benefit from advantages without any proper payment in return.

True patriots will want to obey the law. True patriots, it seems to me, would respond favorably to radio-television programs stressing the necessity of obeying the laws in general and all those special laws that might be cited. Illegal immigrants are automatically excluded from the roster of patriots as are all those, really, who willfully disobey the laws: tax dodgers, bandits, rapists, sneak thieves and the like. All felons are non-patriots.

By means of a radio-television campaign such as I suggest, supported by newspapers, there might well be a renaissance of law observance in the land.

But even if there were no renaissance, there would be no harm in requiring, by law, that radio and television stations put out daily reminders to obey the laws. If it is argued that people would find such reminders boring, it should be noticed that lawyers, judges, prosecutors and police all have intimate knowledge of the laws yet they do not appear to be unduly bored.

As with every suggestion anyone makes, there is, in the United States, an almost automatic objection to it. So it will no doubt be with this suggestion, which probably bears the defect of being well-intentioned.

Some newspaper proprietors may argue that they already in their editorial pages call for observance of all laws. What is irrelevant about this is that people don't want long homilies on the need for law observance. For they already know about that. What they do need, however, is daily reminder, *an aide-memoir*; for in the bustle and hurry of daily affairs they are apt to forget, as Hume well knew.

All people who break the law know they are breaking the law and need no instruction on this score; they do not need to be law professors. This is shown clearly in that most law-breaking takes place in secret or in anticipation of success. Burglars do not openly enter houses; rapists do not commit their assault in full public view; pickpockets do not openly operate.

Law-breaking is committed surreptitiously or, as in the case of bank robbery, is done by surprise with ready means of escape evident. Certain crimes of passion, of course, may be committed openly, in disdain of the law. Those who commit such acts are simply judged to have been carried away by their emotions. It remains a fact that most crimes are committed as secretly as possible, thus showing that those who commit them know they are forbidden, know they are unlawful. They do not need any instruction on this point.

But many of the lesser offenses, committed in many cases out of sheer carelessness, could easily be diminished in number if people were reminded of them. And some of these lesser offenses, like speeding in an automobile, can cause serious harm to others. So I believe it would be of some advantage if people were reminded daily of the necessity to obey the laws.

All societies need such a system of reminders except, perhaps, Japanese society, which is easily the most law-observing society in the world. Although there is corruption in Japan at the top, among politicians and corporate executives, the mass of the public is extremely law-abiding. A western person would be safer walking the streets in any part of Japan in broad daylight than in walking through any of the Third World sections of American cities.

Other names for what I call Third World sections are slums and ghettoes. Such sections are by no means what newspapers call "inner cities," as though they were minute and confined, but are in fact very extensive. In Chicago such sections take in most of the entire South Side and West Side extending to the city limits, at least two-thirds of the city area.

Why are the Japanese so law-abiding and very polite to each other? A big reason is that the population density is 850 people per square mile. This is one of the highest in the world. The population of 124 million, half that of the United States, is crammed into territory slightly smaller than the state of California.

The Japanese, in order to maintain a civilized society, are obliged to be polite. This politeness is a cultural effect and not a natural trait as is shown by the gratuitous cruelty of Japanese troops in their invasions of Asian countries.

In any event, the Japanese are far more orderly than Americans and most other peoples. The cult of freedom, misunderstood, is what leads to much American disorder. The United States is indeed a very free society; there is no doubt of that. But freedom has limits, which is something many Americans simply do not understand. Whenever free action injures or seriously discommodes someone else, it ceases to be freedom and becomes simple tyranny, oppression.

Actually, despite all propaganda about equality before the law, the United States government perpetrates a certain amount of injustice in trying to direct certain behaviors. It does this, for example, by giving subsidies to certain industries and tax discounts to others. By doing this it puts unfavored citizens at specific disadvantages. It may also, through error, bring forth erroneous decisions in the courts. Such decisions are frequent in state courts but are also seen in federal courts.

That many court decisions are wrong and therefore unjust, is evident from the fact that they are so held on appeal. The court system has a built-in corrective mechanism that functions well most of the time. But, occasionally, through error there will be convictions which after many years are overturned in the light of more precise evidence.

Unjust legislation cannot be avoided by those affected. In the United States some of it can be cancelled as unconstitutional. But if it is constitutional it remains on the books, unjust or not. Constitutional injustice is a fact.

Apart from such structural injustice there is the sort of injustice that results, secretly, from corruption. The general taxpayers are charged for all costs of corruption and unnecessary expenditures by the government.

It cannot, therefore, be said that the much-hailed and extravagantly praised United States government produces 100 per cent of justice and equity. Rather does it produce 60, 70 or 80 per cent of justice and equity in society, for which we should be thankful.

As examples of injustice some people point to homeless people and to people in various stages of economic distress or illness. But all such human despair is not chargeable against the government as many people suppose. Many if not most such unfortunates are suffering from self-inflicted injuries—

from drug or alcohol addiction, from having an excess of children they are unable to care for, from various indulgences.

There are, in short, personal aberrations for which the government cannot be held responsible.

But government is a human institution and is therefore subject to error. And people in government function under the same disability as everyone else, being unable to develop as definite a response to the laws as to their personal interests. Government officials are naturally as self-oriented as is the public at large and this is something that experience tells us must be guarded against.

For a concentrated view of the complicated mechanisms used by the United States government to compromise justice and equity for the ordinary masses of its people the reader is referred to a book published in 1992 that is titled *Who Will Tell the People*, by William Greider. Greider, for many years an editor of *The Washington Post*, shows in elaborate detail how in the interplay between government officials and corporations, the general public is often left out in the cold, unprotected against a wide range of corporate-governmental behaviors.

An underlying thesis of Greider is that American democracy has been betrayed. I do not agree that American democracy was ever established. Nor do I, for one, believe that if democracy could be established, it would bring about significant improvements for the common man. For the defect in human nature that we have been examining in this book would make itself apparent in any governmental system.

The only way to overcome this defect is for everybody to obey the law, to the letter, a counsel of perfection that is not apt to be shared by the multitude.

In any event, the people who are truly patriotic are those who obey the laws. For it would be simply idiotic to claim one was patriotic if one consciously broke the laws. All those people who obey the laws can well feel they are patriotic and can censure as unpatriotic those who do not obey the laws.

In view of the vast amount of crime there is in society, there must be many people who are unpatriotic and this is unfortunately true. But those who obey the laws overshadow those who do not. For if it were not a fact that a majority obeyed the laws, society would simply fall apart.

As I said earlier, compliance with the laws can be increased by having the media stress daily, in brief reminders, the necesssity of obeying the laws and to have schools teach the value of laws. What is necessary for the United States is for the public to become more law-conscious, more resolved than ever before to help the government by obeying the laws.

As part of patriotic exercises in the public schools when I was a boy, we used to recite the *Pledge of Allegiance* at the beginning of each day, our right palms placed over our left breast. The pledge ran: "I pledge allegiance to the flag of the United States and to the

Republic for which it stands, one nation indivisible with liberty and justice for all."

This pledge made us all feel very good as we settled down to our lessons.

Since that day, religionists have added the two words "under God" after the words "one nation." What this does is to qualify and restrict the pledge as well as to fasten on it an extraneous description.

What I now propose is that, accepting this amendment, the pledge be further amended to strengthen it.

The pledge I propose would read as follows:

"I pledge allegiance to the flag of the United States and to the Republic for which it stands, one nation indivisible under God or not, with liberty and justice for all."

To my mind such a pledge shows the sort of unqualified loyalty the original pledge was supposed to register and which the first amended pledge does not portray. For, as the "under God" phrase clearly excludes non-believers that pledge weakens the whole.

As far as that goes, the pledge is entirely unofficial, has no public consequences. The oath that public officials take upon assuming office is merely that they will support and defend the Constitution of the United States. That they may take this oath with their hands on the Bible is purely unofficial, a piece of window-dressing for the benefit of the booboisie out in the sticks.

A Note On Government

The United States government is the largest and most complicated apparatus of its kind in the world, easily eclipsing the large former Soviet Union or the old British Empire. As a consequence, many of its deliverances are double-edged, subject to different interpretations.

By and large, however, it delivers whatever there is in its world of justice and equity, at least to the extent of 60 to 80 per cent of each. This, while not perfect, is certainly better than nothing in an imperfect world.

The complexity of the government and the country is shown by the fact that it is a perfect hiding place. So perfect, indeed, is it in this respect, that many former Nazi criminals came to it and remained hidden for long periods. Some have never been discovered. Some may have escaped notice because, like Poe's purloined letter, they remained in full view. In any case, the country never had any difficulty in absorbing Werner von Braun and his rocket crew, quite openly.

The United States is a country and a government of endless possibilities, which is both gratifying and disquieting. This chameleon-like character of the country and the government accounts for the constant cacophony of dissenting voices.

But, although the dollar-cost is high, the government largely fulfills its mission of producing justice and equity.

Here, as an anomaly in the situation let me call attention to the fantastically generous retirement provisions that Congress has voted for members of Congress. Whereas in the corporate world, retirement salary runs at about 30 per cent of base salary (if it exists at all), provisions are so calculated that they may exceed what the Congressman's salary was.

Members of both houses who served when the salary was $60,000 per year (it is now $129,000) now draw more than $60,000 in retirement pay. This result is obtained because, by law, they have cost-of-living allowances that keep them even with inflation at all times. If there were a hyper-inflation their salaries would run into millions of dollars. Again, the lifetime expectancy at the time of retirement envisions a total payout of up to $4 and $5 million. As an observer noted this prospect puts a retiring Congressman from either house of Congress in a position of a person who wins one of the big state lotteries. It puts him and his family on Easy Street for life.

Congressmen point out in semi-rebuttal that they currently pay up to $12,000 per year in retirement fees. Over ten years this would amount to $120,000, far less than the potential benefits a retired congressman could enjoy.

In short, this congressional retirement scheme is a ripoff on the taxpayers, one of many embedded in the government structure. Yet, despite all this, the government is the bulwark of whatever justice and equity there is in the world. If it is not fully satisfactory the task is to improve it, which is something hard to do in the face of all the opposition bound to spring up at the first sign of improvement.

Readers will have seen on television news programs the victory celebrations at political party headquarters after a hard-fought election campaign. Many viewers may well wonder what all the jubiliation and congratulation are about, especially in view of the talk one hears about the cares of office. But if anyone asks what they are celebrating so wildly there is only one answer possible. It is because they know they have struck oil and are on the road to a lifetime of monetary success. In the meantime the champagne glasses clink merrily.

The fact that government is defective in certain respects derives from the fact that people out in society are defective in the way David Hume pointed out: they are not able to bring themselves fully under the rule of law.

Everybody is in the same condition to some extent, some more so than others. Everybody, including government officials, shows the same tendency to shirk adherence to law and equity.

Adherents of the democratic dogma assert that everything would be better if people would pay closer attention to government and foil those who abuse it. But the government is so very complex and extensive that the average person, or even a savant, cannot keep close tabs on it.

Most people must work at least eight hours per

day, sleep eight hours and use the rest of their time tending to personal affairs and going to and from work. Most people have little time to give to watching the government and even specialists who do so cannot take in the whole scene in a lifetime.

There are even historical government episodes that the most learned historians do not know about because the documents relating to them are sealed and immune from the operations of the justly celebrated Freedom of Information Act. So one cannot obtain a full view even of the governmental past. In this respect the government is a closed book.

But, nevertheless, it is the only thing that stands between the populace and the wildest sort of anarchy, complete violence in the streets.

The United States government operates without any outside supervision except from the press, and this supervision is purely informal and sporadic, partial and incomplete.

But here the wisdom of the founders shows itself. No part of the government is under one-man, one-party or one-clique control. The federal government is divided into three parts—legislative, executive and judicial. While there is some cooperation among these parts there is also division of function.

The fifty underlying states are divided in the same way so that there is opportunity to keep an eye on what is going on. The considerable number of governmental scandals that arise shows at least that the system works, perhaps in a clumsy way.

In any event, apart from its high cost the government is able to do its work for the country, perhaps at the level of 60 to 80 per cent and at an extortionate cost. This last is an item the electorate should focus on.

If the electorate doesn't like what it sees, does not like the way Congress votes itself into permanent riches, it should change the composition of Congress and the White House.

The instances of depravity cited in this book are by no means intended to be exhaustive. They are, despite their plenitude, merely representative. For no matter what part of the world one examines one finds the same slippage between mankind's formal intentions and his informal behavior even though not everybody participates to the full in breaking the rules of civilization.